Sexual Violence Policies and Sexual Consent Education at Canadian Post-Secondary Institutions

This book is the culmination of three years of research into sexual violence policies and sexual consent education at post-secondary institutions across Canada. The prevalence of sexual violence has not changed in more than 30 years, and its reporting to police or school authorities has only waxed and waned over those years. In response, this book asks what can be done differently to reduce the number of victims and potential perpetrators?

The book provides an environmental scan of over 120 post-secondary institutions (PSIs) across Canada as well as a deeper analysis of 7 PSIs that also include student and staff experiences and opinions. The three-year research project employed various phases to capture over 160 student voices and over 20 sexual violence staff and subject experts. Subject experts and students were also involved in reviewing the draft iterations of the proposed sexual consent education module. This book delivers readers with a broad-brush approach to understanding the landscape of sexual violence prevention and education services at PSIs across Canada. It provides a narrowed focus on 7 PSIs where student and staff survey responses and interviews provide positionality in response to the available literature. The book concludes with a proposed sexual consent education module, including its strengths and limitations, as a point of discussion for PSIs to include into their sexual violence prevention education repertoire.

This book is intended for post-secondary audiences in Canada, North America, and elsewhere – for undergraduate and graduate students and faculty, staff, and administrators – where it is crucial to consider ways to address its prevalence and the ways we can incorporate prevention education into our campus communities.

D. Scharie Tavcer [she/her] joined Mount Royal University in 2004, where she is now Associate Professor in the Criminal Justice Degree Program. Dr. Tavcer believes in teaching that has components of experiential learning and/ or community service learning. This involves incorporating lived experience into her lectures through guests or off-campus events and providing students with real-world scenarios with real people in real situations. Dr. Tavcer proudly teaches students who wish to enter the criminal justice profession. Many of her students come to university with a narrow view of the world, and others have had some intense lived experiences. But all of them hope to make a difference in the justice system, and she works towards helping them with that goal. Dr. Tavcer's teaching strives to ignite their interest in questioning, reflecting, and addressing the social justice issues within the criminal justice profession. Dr. Tavcer's scholarship approach extends into the social justice arenas of our criminal justice system (CJS). Her work is also intentionally interdisciplinary and intersectional, and she strives for it to be applied research so that the important questions continue to be asked. Dr. Tavcer's scholarship (and teaching) focuses on SV, relationship violence, as well as mental illness and its prevalence in corrections, offender reintegration, criminal law and sentencing, and occupational stress injuries in justice workers. And regardless of the focus, each project aims to be applied research – that the outcome of the research informs practice in some manner.

Vicky Dobkins [she/her] is completing a Master of Arts in Human Security and Peacebuilding at Royal Roads University. She is currently employed as a paralegal at a law firm and a crisis counsellor on the Calgary Sexual Assault Response Team (CSART). Her background includes social work and paramedicine, and she has worked on the front lines in varying capacities for over a decade. Vicky believes in taking a holistic approach when tackling social justice issues and utilising different disciplines as a vehicle for social change. Her personal and professional practice stems from a trauma-informed, anti-oppressive, feminist lens; but above all else, she considers herself a human rights advocate.

"Dr. Tavcer's collection, curation, and consideration of sexual violence policies and sexual consent education at post-secondary institutions across Canada is a necessary contribution to the field of gender-based violence prevention in Canada. I recommend this to those working in the space to learn what else is out there, what has worked, and where we can innovate for safer campus communities."

– **Jake Stika** (he/him), Executive Director, NextGenMen

Sexual Violence Policies and Sexual Consent Education at Canadian Post-Secondary Institutions

D. Scharie Tavcer and Vicky Dobkins

Routledge
Taylor & Francis Group
LONDON AND NEW YORK

First published 2023
by Routledge
4 Park Square, Milton Park, Abingdon, Oxon OX14 4RN

and by Routledge
605 Third Avenue, New York, NY 10158

Routledge is an imprint of the Taylor & Francis Group, an informa business

© 2023 D. Scharie Tavcer and Vicky Dobkins

British Library Cataloguing-in-Publication Data
A catalogue record for this book is available from the British Library

ISBN: 978-1-032-36563-3 (hbk)
ISBN: 978-1-032-36565-7 (pbk)
ISBN: 978-1-003-33267-1 (ebk)

DOI: 10.4324/9781003332671

Typeset in Times New Roman
by Apex CoVantage, LLC

This book is the culmination of three years of research into sexual violence policies and sexual consent education at post-secondary institutions (PSIs) across Canada. Numerous men and women shared their stories and experiences about consent education and with PSIs' responses (or lack thereof) to policies and programming. Regardless of how many research studies or books we complete, the reality remains that sexual violence is pervasive and infiltrates all arenas of life, especially at PSIs, and with people aged 18–25. We need to do better at addressing, educating, and changing our approaches. Thank you to every person who shared their experiences and knowledge and to all folx who are living with sexual violence. This book is for you.

Contents

Figures

Tables

Preface

For years I have been studying sexual violence. It's an issue that divides people in the room. Whenever I tell folx what I research, they dive in, debate, or deflect and walk away. That's okay because I remain passionate about studying sexual violence and I am comfortable with the discomfort.

More recently, the discussions and debates revolve around whether post-secondary institutions (PSIs) should have sexual consent education and if so, should it be mandatory? Many PSIs offer consent education (and other sexual violence programming) on an ad hoc basis to anyone who seeks the info, or it is part of a larger educational programme for resident advisors, student council members, student athletes, and other student leaders. Unfortunately for many PSIs, budget cuts have dissolved prevention programming and staff in these areas.

The prevalence of sexual violence in Canada has not changed in more than 30 years and the reporting of victimisation has only waxed and waned over that same time. In Canada and the United States of America (USA), one in three women over the age of 15 and one in six men have experienced sexual violence during their lifetime. One in five women and one in 16 men are sexually assaulted during their stay at a PSI and more than 90% of those victims do not report to school authorities. The lack of reporting is consistent across North America in that only one in ten sexual assaults is reported to police. In response to these facts, I ask what can be done differently – *what can PSIs do to reduce the number of victims* and *potential perpetrators? What can be done in the face of dwindling budgets and lack of access to programs and services?*

I began my study about sexual consent education by taking an inventory of what is currently offered at over 120 PSIs across Canada. Then I asked students and staff at seven PSIs to explain their understanding of consent, what consent education exists at their university, and who receives that education? And I also asked them if consent education should be mandatory for students and/or mandatory for faculty, staff, and administrators too? If we genuinely want to change prevalence statistics, if we want a campus that provides a safe and violence-free community, if we want an engaged community that includes potential perpetrators, we need to do things differently.

Along with an enthusiastic graduate student, we unpacked the research into these six chapters. The last chapter offers the reader a sexual consent education module. Creating that module was one of the outcomes from this research. It is a culmination of other best practices and educational programming at PSIs in Canada; it is intersectional and inclusive; it is online and interactive; and it addresses rejection, the bystander effect, myth busting, how to talk about consent, and how to support not only people who are victimised but also people who want to take accountability for any harm they have caused. The hope is that it can be added to the repertoire of prevention and education programming at PSIs. The value and need for consent education should no longer be a dividing topic, and an online consent education module should be a welcome addition to campus programming.

Acknowledgements

Thank you to the researchers, academics, students, faculty, and staff across Canada who participated in this research by sharing information, content, completing surveys, and participating in interviews at Mount Royal University (MRU), MacEwan University, University of British Columbia at Okanagan, University of Winnipeg, University of Ottawa, Concordia University, and St. Thomas University. Thank you to people of all genders and identities who live with sexual violence and share their voices, ideas, and experiences. Thank you to the researchers, scholars, and service providers across Canada who contributed knowledge and information to this project.

Thank you to MRU for their support in kind and through grants. Thank you to Royal Roads University for their support through the HUMS Internship Program. Thank you to MRU's Dating, Domestic & Sexual Violence Committee including specialist and advocate, Cari Ionson. Thank you to Dr. Natalie Meisner, TRICO Changemaker, Dr. Emily M. Colpitts, McGill University, Dr. Brianna Wiens, Postdoctoral Fellow, University of Waterloo, the qCollaborative at the University of Waterloo, Dr. Milena Radzikowska at MRU, The Calgary Centre for Sexuality, Calgary Communities Against Sexual Abuse, and NextGenMen.

Abbreviations

2SLGBTQIA+	Two-Spirit, Lesbian, Gay, Bisexual, Trans, Queer, Intersex, Asexual plus
AB	Alberta
BC	British Columbia
BIPs	Bystander intervention programs
BIPOC	Black, Indigenous, and Persons of Colour
CCC	*Criminal Code of Canada*
CFS	Canadian Federation of Students
CJS	Criminal justice system
CSA	Campus sexual assault
CSASA	Campus Sexual Assault Support and Advocacy
DDSVC	Dating, Domestic, and Sexual Violence Committee
GBV	Gender-based violence
GSS	General Social Survey
GWSSA	Graduate Women's Studies Student Association
HRDO	Human Rights and Diversity Office
MB	Manitoba
MRU	Mount Royal University
NB	New Brunswick
NCHA	National College Health Assessment
NFLD	Newfoundland and Labrador
NS	Nova Scotia
NU	Nunavut
NWT	Northwest Territories
ON	Ontario
PEI	Prince Edward Island
PSI	Post-secondary institution(s)
QU	Québec
SARC	Sexual Assault Resource Centre
SK	Saskatchewan

SSPPS	Survey of Safety in Public and Private Spaces
SST	Sexual Script Theory
STU	St. Thomas University
SV	Sexual violence
SVPRO	Sexual Violence Prevention and Response Office
UBCO	University of British Columbia Okanagan
UCR	Uniform Crime Report
UO	University of Ottawa
UofC	University of Calgary
UofT	University of Toronto
USA	United States of America
UW	University of Winnipeg
YK	Yukon

Crediting sources of third-party material

Thank you for sharing content goes to Bow Valley College, University of Victoria, Nova Scotia Community Services, Avalon, Epigeum, Courage to Act, McGill & Concordia Universities, the University of Toronto, and Knowledge One. All other sources are identified within the module including their consent to share and use their content.

1   Introduction to the project

D. Scharie Tavcer

Introduction

When we think about sexual violence (SV) and post-secondary institutions (PSIs) in Canada, one of the things that come to mind is the myriad of cases in the news of how PSIs have failed to provide fulsome prevention, education, or intervention responses when students or staff come forward. We know that post-secondary students are at increased risk of SV, including that racialised and marginalised students are more often targeted. PSI students are most at risk of being targets, and they are also more often perpetrators of SV, and occasionally staff are also victims or perpetrators. PSIs are microcosms of our society – they reflect our population's diversity, represent the good and the bad, and require our conscientious efforts to ensure a campus culture that is free from violence and harassment.

PSIs in Canada

Canada includes 11 provinces and three territories. Post-secondary education is under the auspices of provincial/territorial elected governments and advanced education ministries. Governments are ideologically based and depending on where along the continuum a party sits, investing in post-secondary education may not be a priority. Each budgetary year includes presenting PSIs with their grants – money that offsets the cost of tuition and money that pays for the salaries of its employees, programming and services, utilities, and more. Over the recent years, we are seeing a divesting of funds in post-secondary education programmes and people, which results in some essential services being eliminated or made redundant.

When it comes to SV, only a few provincial governments in Canada have legislated PSIs to create stand-alone SV policies and investigative

DOI: 10.4324/9781003332671-1

procedures (Council of Alberta University Students, 2020; Kindleman, 2020; Shen, 2017). Chapter 4 provides the results from the environmental scan of over 120 PSIs that reveal which PSIs have created stand-alone policies in line with, or despite the absence of legislative directives, while others have SV policies embedded within personal harassment or human rights policies. When legislating policy and programming, governments voice the importance of addressing SV, at least from a liability and investigative perspective, to protect their students and employees.

Many PSIs have robust services available for students (less so for employees) that include consent education and other SV education programming and support. Many PSIs offer SV education programming on an ad hoc basis to anyone who seeks the info. Some PSIs even have dedicated sexual assault or women centres, counselling, and health services, where support, education, and programming are offered. Over the decades, attention to SV at PSIs has increased markedly, but aside from that, the prevalence of SV in Canada has not changed in over 30 years, and neither has how we deal with it. It remains one of the most under-reported criminal offences in Canada (Cotter, 2021; Department of Justice, 2019; Sheehy, 2012), and studies at PSIs reveal that students do not choose to report to PSI officials for distinct reasons (Ahmed, 2021; Spencer et al., 2017). Further exacerbating reporting rates and support for students and employees is that some provinces have slashed budgets and grants to PSIs, which results in the closing of services, positions, or a reduction in programming in these key areas.

The project

In response to the realities outlined earlier, we ask what can be done differently. What can PSIs do to reduce the number of victims *and* potential perpetrators? What can be done in the face of dwindling budgets and access to programs and services that are not available 24/7? How can consent education be more accessible and could mandatory prevention education work towards increasing reporting and reducing prevalence?

This book is based on nearly three years of research into the policies that address SV, and the consent education programming offered at PSIs across Canada. This research involved scanning, collating, and analysing data at over 120 PSIs. The project also included over 160 interviews and surveys collected from students, staff, and service providers at various PSIs and communities across Canada. Two objectives guided the project: Conduct an environmental scan of what's being offered, and listen to students, staff, and experts.

Method

This book is based on a research project that involved scanning PSIs across Canada between 2019 and 2021. The project included quantitative and qualitative methods and was partially impacted by the COVID-19 pandemic in that in-person face-to-face interviews at PSIs were halted and an electronic recruitment and data collection method replaced that.

The guiding questions of the study were as follows:

- To gather information about policies and services at PSIs.
- To gather students' definitions of consent and their opinions about consent education.
- To review consent education practices across Canada.
- To explore the benefits and limitations of online consent education.
- To understand the benefits and limitations of mandatory consent education.

Information about SV and consent education came from various expert sources, students, staff, academic, government, and grey literature, Statistics Canada, scholarly studies, and the Canadian universities' National College Health Assessment. The results worked towards creating an online sexual consent module to add to the repertoire of prevention and education programming.

The research project involved several phases within its methodology. As with any research study, this project had limitations. The COVID-19 pandemic limited the depth and breadth of collecting data. Face-to-face interviews produce rich narratives and data that allow the researcher to explore tangents and deeper meaning (Dialsingh, 2008; Jamshed, 2014; Oltman, 2016). Whereas electronic recruitment and surveys can produce data that in some ways is more truthful than face-to-face interviews as participants feel more comfortable (Dworkin et al., 2016; McInroy, 2016). Although electronic surveys are a valid data collection method (Dawson, 2019; Regmi et al., 2016; Wyatt, 2000), they are not without challenges. Convincing students to participate in research can be a challenge while they juggle the demands of their personal lives, course work, and deadlines. Further challenges include the ease and accessibility of completing surveys, and whether the topic or the incentive is suitably motivating.

Other limitations include that due to the time and location of this research, the results cannot be generalised to every PSI across Canada. In addition, by the time of publication, some of the PSIs may have addressed their lack of policy and accessibility to services.

Phase 1

The research project was divided into phases. Phase 1 involved using content analysis to code information from an environmental scan of 130 PSIs across Canada. The analysis included collating whether the PSI has a stand-alone SV policy and protocol; whether it has an SV centre or other support services related to education, prevention, and interventions for SV; whether it offers consent education, and if so, is it on an ad hoc basis; is it online, in person, or both; and whether their consent education programming is mandatory and for whom.

Concurrently, temporary access was obtained to complete existing consent education online modules currently delivered at various PSIs. Completing those modules included a content analysis of language, design, topics, and interactions, then a summation and critique of its content and interface. These included the following: McGill University's (Québec) *It Takes All of Us*; University of Toronto's (Ontario) *Sexual Violence Education and Prevention Module*; Bow Valley College's (Alberta) *Supporting Disclosure of Sexual Violence Training for Students*; the Nova Scotia Sexual Violence Strategy's *Supporting Survivors of Sexual Violence;* and Epigeum's *Consent Matters*.

Phase 1 also included a literature review. With the support of two student research assistants, the literature review included scholarly, legal, government, and grey literature under the themes of SV in PSIs; athletics and SV at PSIs; bystander interventions and programming; legal cases relating to SV and consent in Canada; literature pertaining to toxic masculinity, misogyny, rape culture; rape myths; dealing with rejection; responses to SV; racialised violence, consent, consent education, and the pros and cons of mandating education; and SV prevalence in Canada and at PSIs.

Phase 2

From the 130 PSIs, seven were chosen for in-person interviews with students and staff (from their respective SV centres or staff who deliver SV education and prevention programming). These seven PSIs varied in size from coast to coast and included St. Thomas University (New Brunswick); Concordia University (Québec); University of Ottawa (Ontario); University of Winnipeg (Manitoba); MacEwan University and Mount Royal University (Alberta); and the University of British Columbia Okanagan (British Columbia). Ethics approval was received from each with a travel plan for the spring of 2020. Data collection began in New Brunswick at the start of March 2020, but once the COVID-19 pandemic hit, it forced the shutdown of all public spaces including universities. Data collection was suspended and later revised to an online recruitment and collection strategy. Ethics approval for these revisions was granted to permit electronic recruitment over social media at these seven PSIs.

We recruited participants during April–May 2020, September–December 2020, and January–March 2021. We posted the recruitment link to the anonymous electronic survey on the seven universities' social media and student association or student group accounts (with permission), and on Dr. Tavcer's Twitter, Facebook, and LinkedIn accounts with relevant hashtags and tags.

The survey asked participants if they were over the age 18 and stated that underage participants may choose to complete this survey, but their responses will not be included in the study. In total, 169 students completed interviews and the survey with an uneven distribution of participants among the seven PSIs.

An additional 24 interviews with SV staff at PSIs were conducted for insight into their experiences and expertise in their prevention and education programming and services. These individuals were from the seven PSIs and from the University of Victoria, the University of Calgary, Concordia University, University of British Columbia Okanagan, the Centre for Sexuality, and the Avalon Sexual Assault Centre Nova Scotia. We also interviewed security service staff, residence advisors and staff, student council executives, members from the Council of Alberta University Students, SV treatment and programming staff, and community service providers.

Phase 3

In addition to the dissemination of the research findings, another goal was to create an online sexual consent education module. The vision was that such a module would be a culmination of the research project's findings in the form of an accessible, intersectional, online, and interactive consent education module. The module was a culmination of all data collected. There is a tremendous amount of excellent content and programming already available across Canada in the form of online modules, handouts, videos, in-person workshops, and more. The online module combines these best practices into a 60-minute interactive module that hits the most salient pieces directed at an audience of post-secondary students.

A consultation on the draft table of contents for the proposed module occurred with experts and stakeholders at three different points in time. The table of contents was generated from collating the findings from interviews, surveys, and other modules and online content.

At the start of the project, the draft table of contents of the curriculum for the consent education module was shared with experts, scholars, service providers, and advocates from NextGenMen, The Centre for Sexuality, Calgary Communities Against Sexual Abuse, and subject expert scholars from McGill University, the University of Toronto, and Mount Royal University. Unfortunately, our invitation for feedback from educators who work in Indigenous communities was not returned.

Feedback from participating stakeholders was sought a second and third time (in the beginning and end of 2021). First when the module's content was curated in its initial draft and again when the table of contents was finalised. Their expertise with clients and front-line perspectives allowed for a robust review of the consent education module and critique of its content, depth and breadth, and its user interface.

When a definitive version of the table of contents was confirmed, the module's content was finalised. Then two information design experts applied a design aesthetic to the entire module and critiqued and corrected its user interface where needed. Once complete, additional input was sought from a group of randomly selected students. They were asked to go through the online module and answer online survey questions critiquing its interface and providing feedback about the content.

The module

This book presents a culmination of the research project as well as presents an online sexual consent education module for post-secondary students. The module is portable, accessible, and intersectional. The module accentuates systemic cultural issues that sustain violence, how to confront power dynamics, and how to support others. The audience includes everyone – even those who may perpetuate violence and how to support those who seek accountability for their actions. It redirects the discussion away from "how not to get assaulted" towards how we can shift the culture at PSIs to prevent violence and enrich a #cultureofconsent.

The book serves as a resource to know what is happening (or not happening) across Canadian PSIs and to support similar projects at PSIs outside of Canada. It can also serve as a tool for policymakers and administrative leaders at PSIs who wish to make change, and as a resource for staff, professionals, and practitioners to support the need and funding for their work.

There is a multitude of literature debating efficacious pedagogy and the merits and limitations of mandatory education. There are arguments to both sides of the debate. The data support the position that sexual consent education and prevention programming need to stand on the side of modernity – the contemporary way in which students today access and absorb information. Online and mandatory sexual consent education is necessary because, despite decades of violence prevention, education campaigns, protests, legislative changes, and prevention programming, the prevalence rates of SV have not changed in Canada for over 30 years. The reporting rates of SV have not drastically changed in Canada for over 30 years. What we have been doing has not shifted our culture away from a rape culture towards a #cultureofconsent. Prevention programming over the past decades has remained focused on warning potential victims. Most programming and educational efforts over the past decades have not incorporated intersectional perspectives or tackled toxic masculinity, colonialism, and patriarchy. Most programming and educational efforts over the past decades have not spoken directly to potential perpetrators.

An online sexual consent education module can be an *additional* form of consent education added to the repertoire of existing prevention and education programming. This suggestion is not to proclaim that an online sexual consent education module will be the panacea to changing rape culture and eliminating SV, or that it should replace other programming or campaigns. The suggestion here is to include an online sexual consent education module as an additional part of the education, prevention, and intervention repertoire at PSIs and to consider making it mandatory.

Students (and employees) are mandated to take other programming such as cybersecurity awareness, first aid, or general education coursework at PSIs. As educational institutions that extol the merits of lifelong learning, why is it not possible to add consent education to students' educational journeys? Mandating such training would work towards ensuring that all sorts of students are aware of its importance – often only the converted show up to events, campaigns, committees, and initiatives that deal with SV. To sustain a #cultureofconsent, PSIs need to reach everyone in every corner of campus to truly make a difference in prevention and prevalence.

Unique and innovative

This book considers consent education in a way that meets the reality of education in the 21st century. From interviews and surveys with students, staff, and stakeholders, the merits and limitations of consent-based education were debated. Also considered were the merits and limitations of mandatory education, using existing discussions in the literature as a starting point. The results overwhelmingly favour online education that is not only mandatory for students but also mandatory for everyone on campus.

Prevention programming at PSIs needs to shift, pivot, or flip, because university-aged men and women are over-represented as targets of SV, and despite decades of violence prevention, education campaigns, and programming, the prevalence and reporting rates have not lessened. A modern, online, intersectional kind of consent education needs to be added to the existing repertoire of prevention and education programming.

Extending on previous research and scholarship about SV, consent, consent education, online education, and mandatory education, we combined this with data from the study. The data from students, staff, and stakeholders, provides evidence that supports looking at consent education in a new way.

Using existing discussions in the literature as a starting point and the research collected in this project, the book concludes with the proposed online sexual consent education module. Creating it was a culmination of all the data collected (student, staff, and stakeholder input, student feedback and input on the module's iterations, prevalence data, the environmental scan, and literature about consent education and mandatory education). Design experts helped create an aesthetically pleasing module that could be adapted for use in any PSI. This module version is directed at students. Future versions could be adapted for faculty and staff learners. And consideration could be given to revising the module for students in grades 7–12 in the public education systems.

The following chapters build a foundation of support for the online module. Chapter 1 was an introduction to the research project including its methods, benefits, and limitations. Chapter 2 unpacks the discourse about why SV rates have not changed in over 30 years while also providing the statistical reality of SV in Canada, including solidifying our understanding of the systemic issues that create and sustain SV. Provoking our understanding of consent education, how the current practices at PSIs align (or not) with the literature on consent education, and the pros and cons of mandatory education are presented in Chapter 3. Findings from the environmental scan of PSIs' policies and programming are presented in Chapter 4. Findings from student and staff participants about consent and consent education are presented in Chapter 5. And the book concludes with a summary of the online sexual consent education module in Chapter 6.

References

Ahmed, S. (2021). *Complaint!* Duke University Press.

Dawson, C. (2019). *Introduction to research methods 5th edition: A practical guide for anyone undertaking a research project.* Robinson.

Cotter, A. (2021, August 25). Criminal victimization in Canada, 2019. *Canadian Centre for Justice and Community Safety Statistics.* https://www150.statcan.gc.ca/n1/pub/85-002-x/2021001/article/00014-eng.htm

Council of Alberta University Students. (2020). *CAUS releases campus sexual violence white paper.* www.caus.net/news/2020/2/10/caus-releases-campus-sexual-violence-white-paper

Department of Justice. (2019, April). *Just facts: Sexual assault.* www.justice.gc.ca/eng/rp-pr/jr/jf-pf/2019/apr01.html

Dialsingh, I. (2008). Face-to-face interviewing. In P. J. Lavrakas (Ed.), *Encyclopedia of survey research methods* (pp. 276–261). Sage Publications, Inc. https://dx.doi.org/10.4135/9781412963947.n174

Dworkin, J., Hessel, H., Gliske, K., & Rudi, J. H. (2016). A comparison of three online recruitment strategies for engaging parents. *Family Relations, 65*(4), 550–561. https://doi.org/10.1111/fare.12206

Jamshed, S. (2014). Qualitative research method-interviewing and observation. *Journal of Basic and Clinical Pharmacy, 5*(4), 87–88. https://doi.org/10.4103/0976-0105.141942

Kindleman, T. (2020, February 10). Report calls for province to develop sexual violence policy for universities. *CBC News.* www.cbc.ca/news/canada/edmonton/u-of-a-sexual-violence-report-1.5457775

McInroy, L. B. (2016). Pitfalls, potentials, and ethics of online survey research: LGBTQ and other marginalized and hard-to-access youths. *Social Work Research 40*(2), 83–94. https://doi.org/10.1093/swr/svw005

Oltman, S. M. (2016). Qualitative interviews: A methodological discussion of the interviewer and respondent contexts. *Forum Qualitative Social Research, 17*(2). www.qualitative-research.net/index.php/fqs/article/view/2551/3998

Regmi, P. R., Waithaka, E., Paudyal, A., Simkhada, P., & van Teijlingen, E. (2016). Guide to the design and application of online questionnaire surveys. *Nepal Journal of Epidemiology, 6*(4), 640–644. https://doi.org/10.3126/nje.v6i4.17258

Sheehy, E. A. (Ed.). (2012). *Sexual assault in Canada: Law, legal practice and women's activism.* Les Presses de l'Université d'Ottawa | University of Ottawa Press. http://books.openedition.org/uop/535

Shen, A. (2017, August 4). Universities across Canada implement sexual violence policies. *University Affairs.* www.universityaffairs.ca/news/news-article/universities-across-canada-implement-sexual-violence-policies/

Spencer, C., et al. (2017). Why sexual assault survivors do not report to universities: A feminist analysis: Reporting sexual assault. *Journal of Family Relations, 66*(1), 166–179. https://doi.org/10.1111/fare.12241

Wyatt, J. C. (2000). When to use web-based surveys. *Journal of the American Medical Informatics Association: JAMIA, 7*(4), 426–429. https://doi.org/10.1136/jamia.2000.0070426

2   Sexual violence in Canada

Vicky Dobkins and D. Scharie Tavcer

Introduction

Sexual violence (SV) is a widespread issue in Canada, and its prevalence rates have remained stagnant for the last 30+ years. The fact that it is a common occurrence (with approximately one in three women and one in six men expected to experience SV at some point in their life) (Conroy & Cotter, 2017; Senn et al., 2014) is not readily accepted, nor should it be. In Canada, one in five women and one in sixteen men experience SV during their stay at a post-secondary institution (PSI) (Fisher et al., 2010). Across Canada and the United States of America (USA), one in three women and one in six men over the age of 15 have experienced SV during their lifetime (Benoit et al., 2015; Cantalupo, 2016; Fisher et al., 2010; Holland & Cortina, 2017; Karjane et al., 2002; Krebs et al., 2007; Morgan & Truman, 2017; Tjaden & Thoeness, 2000; United States Department of Justice, 2005), and in over 80% of cases, victims and perpetrators know each other (Burczycka, 2020; Cotter, 2021; Khan & Sweet, 2020).

SV is a social justice and human rights issue that should be at the forefront of our most pressing social concerns. At first glance, SV may seem like a straightforward concept that describes an individual being coerced into a sexual act against their will, but this oversimplified perception is somewhat inaccurate. SV has many intricacies that make it an incendiary and polarising topic, evidenced in the misunderstanding of what it and consent are. Although the content of this book centres on SV within the context of PSIs, it is imperative to expose the serious and significant impacts that SV has on our entire population. This chapter intends to deconstruct the term *sexual violence* and evaluate the systemic factors that contribute to its prevalence in Canada. It aims to enable the reader to build on their knowledge of SV by providing an overview of the intersectional elements presented in current research and literature.

DOI: 10.4324/9781003332671-2

A note about language

Language is remarkably powerful, but its capability to shape or skew individuals' perceptions is vastly underestimated. Historically, the language surrounding SV has been stated to be an ideological battleground that has subsequently utilised narrow definitions to err on the side of caution (Grady, 2017). These narrow definitions were often gendered and positioned within a heteronormative framework where SV was a crime perpetrated solely by men against women. This gendered view of SV implored a detrimental use of language that ascribed blame onto victims and minimised a perpetrator's responsibility. This use of language has been acknowledged as limited and insufficient in addressing the nuances and complexities of SV. Thankfully, the language surrounding SV is evolving to reflect a new vocabulary that is inclusive, purposeful, and bolsters the reduction of existing stigmas.

It is important to note that the use of language is contextual and is often informed by varying disciplines, theories, approaches, evidence-based practice, and a person's experiences. For example, a trauma-informed approach uses language to prevent triggering, minimalising, or trivialising an individual's experience of SV. A trauma-informed approach employs the use of person-first language as it prioritises the person first and the characteristics as secondary (i.e., a person who has experienced violence or a person who has been targeted). Care and attention need to be given to language in developing resources or policies surrounding SV. Language can reflect the gravity of an issue and will shape how it is discussed. Many researchers agree that the language used to name a problem is significant to the various social, political, and legal responses to the phenomenon (Aghtaie & Ganjoli, 2015; Buss et al., 2016; Humphreys & Towl, 2020; Merry, 2009; Nelson, 2017). As SV is a sensitive subject for some and a highly traumatic topic for others, specific terminology has elicited ongoing debates throughout various disciplines (e.g., the use of survivor instead of victim).

The term *survivor* is often the preferred term utilised by practitioners and advocates in efforts to empower and honour the strength, courage, and resilience of those who have experienced SV. In contrast, *victim* is a term often used when describing a person who has been subjected to a crime and is commonly used in numerous resources, policies, and pieces of legislation. Individuals who have experienced SV may identify as a survivor, victim, as both, and identify with something else entirely. Is one term better than the other? It is recognised and accepted that an individual who has experienced SV has the right to choose how they wish to identify themselves. Still, for this text that presents aggregate data, the term *victim* is used and *perpetrator* to denote a person who has committed the act of SV.

Within the context of the legal system, the language surrounding SV is situated within the criminal justice system's (CJS's) ideology with terms such as *complainant* or *witness*, which refers to a person who reports their victimisation to the police. The term *offender* is used in the CJS when referring to a person convicted in a court of law and/or incarcerated. Someone arrested or charged with a criminal offence, such as sexual assault, is often labelled with the term *accused*; someone on trial for this criminal offence is often labelled the *defendant*.

The language surrounding SV within the context of criminal case law is complicated because it both sets a precedent for legal definitions and is influential in creating or reinforcing societal attitudes. This can be problematic because the language used cannot be easily amended within the legal context or in statutes. If a change is to be made, it is often reflected in theory or policy, not practice. An example of this is emulated through the terms *rape* and *sexual assault*. These are standard default terms used to identify sexual acts committed against a person who does not or cannot consent (Armstrong et al., 2018). Although often used interchangeably, they are significantly different from one another. They do not reflect the evolutive nature of our understanding of SV and the many ways in which it can be performed. This is illustrated through the evolution of both terms as they are defined in the *Criminal Code of Canada*.

Rape versus sexual assault

The *Criminal Code of Canada* is a federal statute that was first enacted in 1892 and includes definitions of criminal offences created by the Parliament of Canada (Government of Canada, 2021). In 1892, the *Criminal Code* included the offence of *rape*, which was narrowly defined as a man having non-consensual sexual intercourse (referred to as carnal knowledge) with a woman who was not his wife. The act of carnal knowledge was considered complete "upon penetration to any, even the slightest degree, and even without the emission of seed" (*Criminal Code*, R.S.C., 1892, c. 174, s. 266). Those guilty of the offence could face life in prison (Lakin Afolabi Law, 2022; Somerville & Gall, 2012). Interestingly, the etymology of the term *rape* comes from the Latin word *rapere*, which refers to the seizure, theft, or abduction of property (EVABC, 2016). This exemplifies patriarchal beliefs and practices that women were the property of their husbands, and in essence, the laws against rape were created to protect a man's property interests and maintain male social dominance (Lakin Afolabi Law, 2022; Armstrong et al., 2018). Common law rule also stated that a man could not rape his wife because she had perpetually consented to sexual intercourse as part of the marriage contract. Other problematic aspects of the rape offence centred on components of gender and sexuality set within a heterosexual lens – perpetrators of rape were exclusively men, and women were exclusively victims; subsequently, female sexuality was defined by male sexuality.

Ninety years later, Canadian rape laws were reformed with the implementation of Bill C-127, *An Act to Amend the Criminal Code in Relation to Sexual Offences and Other Offences Against the Person* (1983). These reforms made several changes to repeal the discriminatory rape offence provisions prompted by low reporting levels and the stigma associated with sexual assault (Kong et al., 2003; Lakin Afolabi Law, 2022; Somerville & Gall, 2012). Advocates working to eradicate SV influenced the statute in that society and lawmakers finally recognised that sexual assault was not a crime of sex but rather a crime for power and control over another. One focus of the new sexual assault provisions was to encourage reporting and to improve the CJS response to reports (Kong et al., 2003; Primeau, n.d.). A gender-neutral language was employed, and spousal immunity was repealed, meaning that a person could be charged with sexual assault against their spouse (Biesenthal, 1991; Kong et al., 2003; Mewett, 1993). The offences of rape were repealed from the *Criminal Code* and replaced with a three-tiered offence structure of sexual assault offences that captured a much broader range of conduct (*Criminal Code*, RSC 1985, c. C-46, ss. 271–273; Davison, 2016). See Box 2.1.

Box 2.1: Three sexual assault offences from the *Criminal Code of Canada*.

Section 271: **Sexual assault** is an offence considered to be any non-consensual act that violates the sexual integrity of another person.

Section 272: **Sexual assault with a weapon, threats to a third party or causing bodily harm** is an offence when a person is sexually assaulted by a perpetrator with a weapon or who uses an imitation weapon or threatens to use a weapon and causes bodily harm. Or the perpetrator threatens harm directed at the victim or a third party.

Section 273: **Aggravated sexual assault** is an offence when a person is sexually assaulted and the perpetrator wounds, maims, disfigures, beats the victim, or the victim is in danger of losing their life because of being sexually assaulted.

Source: Authors.

Sections 271–273 describe three escalating levels of sexual assault offences but fail to provide a standardised definition of sexual assault other than non-consensual conduct of a sexual nature. The term *assault*, however, is defined in the statute under Section 26. It is described as the *intentional application of force to another person (whether directly or indirectly) without the consent of that person*. In theory, Section 271 can be interpreted to include non-consensual behaviour such as kissing, touching, fondling, and penetration of any kind, in any place, by any part of the body or foreign instrument. But in practice, charging and prosecuting perpetrators for non-consensual kissing or touching does not often occur due to understaffed prosecution services and possible unwillingness due to stereotypes and patriarchal ideologies.

A few years later, a standardised definition of *sexual assault* was determined in *R. v. Chase* [1987], 2 S.C.R. 293 as "an assault which is committed in circumstances of a sexual nature, such that the sexual integrity of the victim is violated" (para. 3). The phrase "the sexual integrity of the victim is violated" is incorporated into the interpretation of the statute. In making this determination and establishing the act element of sexual assault, the court held that the evidence must show the following:

(1)   A touching of the complainant by the accused.
(2)   The sexual nature of that contact.
(3)   The absence of the complainant's consent.

The first two elements are objective, but the third element – the absence of consent – is determined by the victim/complainant's internal state of mind at the time the criminal offence occurred and is, therefore, subjective (CICS, 2018; Kong et al., 2003; Scott, 2017). Two crucial aspects of this third element are the inclusion of consent (which will be elaborated upon in the next chapter) and the determination of evidence from the victim's perspective. This is especially significant as sexual assault laws have been historically implemented on the basis of formal legal rules and informal assumptions. A victim's perspective had never previously been considered; instead, it was usually met with deep suspicion.

In 1992, the *Criminal Code* (under Bill C-49) was amended to include other legal measures (Section 276: evidence of complainant's sexual activity, commonly known as rape shield laws) in an attempt to eradicate the use of discriminatory beliefs in court proceedings and to block overt expressions of victim blaming (Craig, 2016, 2018; Shaffer, 2012). Before the inclusion of S. 276, a victim's sexual history could be used to discredit them as a witness/complainant in court. Despite its intention, the law continues to engage sexual assault myths and stereotypes, intimidated, and discouraged victims from coming forward, and discredited their experience if they had a sexual history.[1]

Section 276 forbids including evidence that a complainant has engaged in sexual activity (with the accused or any other person) and restricts questions about that individual's prior sexual activity except under specific circumstances with a court application to justify their inclusion (EVABC, 2016). These reforms challenged myths and stereotypes such that prior sexual activity means the complainant is "more likely to have consented to the sexual activity that forms the subject-matter of the charge;" or "is less worthy of belief" (S.276.1(a)(b)). These reforms are continually revisited and reviewed, but despite the advances made, prevailing biases and sexist ideologies ingrained in the CJS practices continue (Craig, 2016; 2018). These create barriers for individuals impacted by SV. Like all laws, the sexual assault provisions are only as good as their implementation in practice.

The definitions of *rape* and *sexual assault* are distinguishable from each other but remain synonymous with how society discusses and understands these laws. The *Criminal Code* of today (2022) defines three sexual assault offences involving adult complainants (sexual offences against children are found in Sections 151–155, 160, and 170–173), which is an improvement from the inception of these laws. However, it remains imperative to acknowledge that Canadian laws are rooted in colonial, patriarchal, and misogynist ideologies with limitations surrounding gender, sexuality, identity, myths, and stereotypes that have yet to be fully addressed equally in the way the law is written, interpreted, and understood by society.

Later in 1999, another Supreme Court ruling contributed to our understanding of sexual assault. In *R. v. Ewanchuk* [1999] 1 S.C.R. 330, the court confirmed that a conviction for sexual assault requires proof beyond reasonable doubt that the accused committed acts of unwanted sexual touching and that their intention to touch was without consent from the person being touched. *Ewanchuk* confirmed the three elements to define sexual assault: (i) touching, (ii) the sexual nature of the contact, and (iii) the absence of consent.

Sexual violence

SV is not just another term to describe sexual assault, and it is not a term codified in the statute (Benoit et al., 2015; Cotter & Savage, 2019). It is an over-arching, non-legal term incorporating various sexual thoughts, actions, and verbal and written conduct. SV is a term that has evolved through the advocacy, education, and prevention work done by front-line service providers, scholars, and experts who study its reality. It is often referred to as an umbrella term because of the wide range of concepts and forms of violence it encompasses, which is why its cultural significance and definitions have been long contested (Armstrong et al., 2018). SV is a social justice issue rooted in systems of power, privilege, and oppression that are differently distributed among people of differing identities (Hong & Marine, 2018).

Violence committed against someone based on their gender identity, gender expression, or perceived gender, also known as gender-based violence (GBV), encompasses a range of behaviours that stems from gender inequality and unequal power relationships (WHO & PAHO, 2012; Women & Gender Equality Canada, 2018). SV can constitute any sexual act that targets a person's sexuality or gender identity and expression, regardless of whether the action is physical or psychological. SV describes acts that extend far beyond physically forced penetration and can include all forms of conduct that is sexual in nature and is unwanted, coerced, and committed without consent (Basile et al., 2014; Cook et al., 2018).

Academics and service providers describe SV as conduct that ranges from thoughts to jokes, verbal or behavioural sexual harassment, non-consensual sharing of explicit images electronically or in person, unwanted exposure to sexual situations, stalking, voyeurism, exploitation, verbal and nonverbal expressions of rape culture, being exposed to unwanted sexual images electronically, or in person, and more (Basile et al., 2014; Cook et al., 2018). SV exists on a continuum of expression and is the evolutionary sum of its numerous values and behaviours. This continuum includes thoughts, words, actions, and behaviours that range from being subtle, such as talking about women as sexual objects, to overt acts, such as sexual assault at a party (SVPC, 2017). Incidents of sexism or expressions of rape culture are too often dismissed, depicting a lack of understanding of being on the continuum of violence. All values and behaviours on the continuum are harmful, with even the most subtle forms of microaggressions having the power to reinforce inequality and exert power and control over another.

Sexual violence statistics

In Canada, it is estimated that there are more than 940,000 sexual assaults per year (Cotter, 2021), which equates to almost two (1.8) sexual assaults every minute of every day for an entire year. In 2018, more than 11 million Canadians (representing 37% of the population 15 years of age and older) reported, they had experienced a physical or sexual assault since age 15 (Cotter & Savage, 2019; Rotenberg, 2017a). Crime and victimisation statistics are derived through two primary national surveys: The Uniform Crime Reporting (UCR) Survey and the General Social Survey (GSS) on Canadians' Safety (victimisation). Statistics Canada developed the UCR Survey, and its census includes individuals of all ages and covers approximately

99% of the population (Conroy & Cotter, 2017; Moreau, 2022). The UCR collects crime statistics and documents a measure of crime that is *police-reported* (Kong et al., 2003).

In contrast to the UCR, the GSS on victimisation provides information on specific policy issues of current or emerging interest and is conducted every five years, with the most recent cycle completed in 2019 (Kong et al., 2003; Moreau, 2022). Victimisation surveys provide an alternative to police statistics in that they interview victims directly about their experiences of crime and therefore include both incidents that are reported to the police and those that are not. It has been well documented that only a small portion of all crimes are reported to the police, so self-reported surveys are a valuable supplement to official police reports (Conroy & Cotter, 2017; Moreau, 2022). The earliest UCR crime statistics on police-reported sexual assaults were made available after reform legislation in 1983 (see Figure 2.1). Police-reported sexual assaults only include incidents reported to and classified as *founded* crimes by police, so these statistics represent a small fraction of the true extent of the prevalence of sexual assaults (Rotenberg, 2017a).

The rates of police-reported sexual assaults are correlated with significant changes to sexual assault legislation and social movements. After reforms to rape legislation (with the implementation of Bill C-127 in 1983), there were notable increases in police-reported sexual offences that peaked in 1992 and 1993 when rape shield laws were introduced (Sheehy, 2000; Rotenberg, 2017a; Tang, 1998). The emergence of the #MeToo social movement in

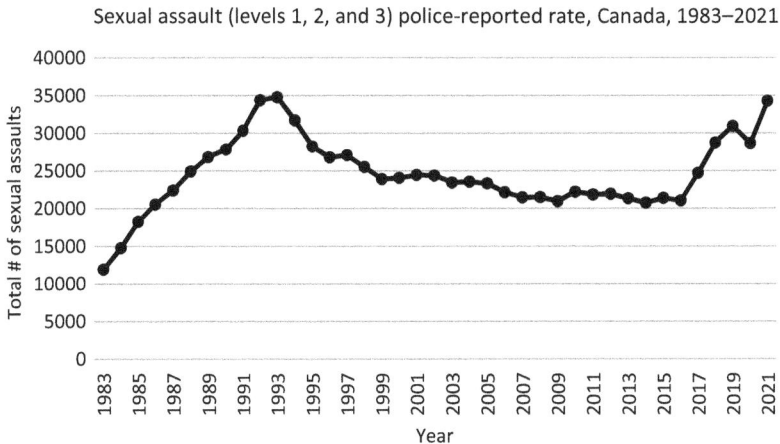

Figure 2.1 Police-reported sexual assaults from 1983 to 2021.

Source: Adapted from Statistics Canada.

2017 sparked public discussion around SV and misconduct, prompting an increase in the number of sexual assaults reported to police (Conroy, 2018; Cotter & Savage, 2019; Rotenberg & Cotter, 2018).

In addition, police also renewed their commitment to review their response to accusations of sexual assault and to revisit files previously classified as *unfounded* (Doolittle et al., 2017; Canadian Centre for Justice Statistics, 2018; Greenland & Cotter, 2018). But despite the increased societal awareness, data from victimisation surveys conducted between 1993 and 2019 showed that the rate of self-reported sexual assaults remained relatively stable (see Figure 2.2) (Besserer & Trainor, 2000; Conroy & Cotter, 2017; Perreault, 2015; Rotenberg, 2017a). Notably, the rates for other types of self-reported violent and non-violent crime declined during this time (Conroy & Cotter, 2017; Perreault, 2015).

Under-reported

Research has widely documented that for many reasons, sexual assault is one of the most under-reported crimes in Canada (Benoit et al., 2015; Brennan & Taylor-Butts, 2008; Conroy & Cotter, 2017; Cotter & Savage, 2019; Kaufman, 2008; Luce et al., 2010; Rotenberg, 2017a). As most incidents of sexual assault are not reported to the police, they are not captured by the UCR. For this reason, self-reported information collected by the GSS on victimisation provides further insight into the nature and extent of sexual

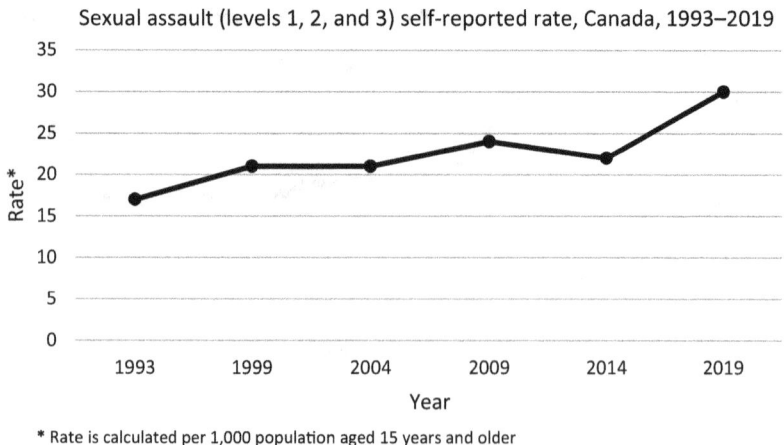

Sexual assault (levels 1, 2, and 3) self-reported rate, Canada, 1993–2019

* Rate is calculated per 1,000 population aged 15 years and older

Figure 2.2 Self-reported sexual assaults from 1993 to 2019.

Source: Adapted from Statistics Canada.

assault in Canada (Conroy & Cotter, 2017). Notably, the odds of sexual assault being reported to police are about 80% lower than other violent crimes (Cotter, 2021).

The 2019 GSS on victimisation[2] shows that only 6% of sexual assaults were brought to the attention of the police (see Figure 2.3) (Cotter, 2021), a rate that is comparatively lower than in earlier years of other self-reported surveys (Conroy, 2021; Conroy & Cotter, 2017; Cotter & Savage, 2019; Rotenberg & Cotter, 2018).

Among all crimes reported to the police, a certain number are deemed unfounded. This occurs when a police investigation determines that the offence reported did not occur, nor was it attempted (Greenland & Cotter, 2018; Statistics Canada, 2016). In 2017, 14% of sexual assaults (levels 1, 2, and 3) reported to police were classified as unfounded, meaning that police determined just under 3,900 incidents of sexual assault not to have taken place (Greenland & Cotter, 2018). As mentioned earlier, media reports on the differences in how police classify sexual assaults as founded or unfounded resulted in reviews by police and a renewed commitment to victims (Doolittle, 2017; Doolittle et al., 2017; Canadian Association of Chiefs of Police, 2017; Greenland & Cotter, 2018).

New UCR Survey standards for classifying incidents as founded or unfounded were updated in January 2018 to reflect a more victim-centred approach. This approach puts forth that unless there is concrete evidence to prove the crime did not happen, it is to be believed that the crime occurred,

Percentage of sexual assaults reported to police, Canada, 1993–2019*

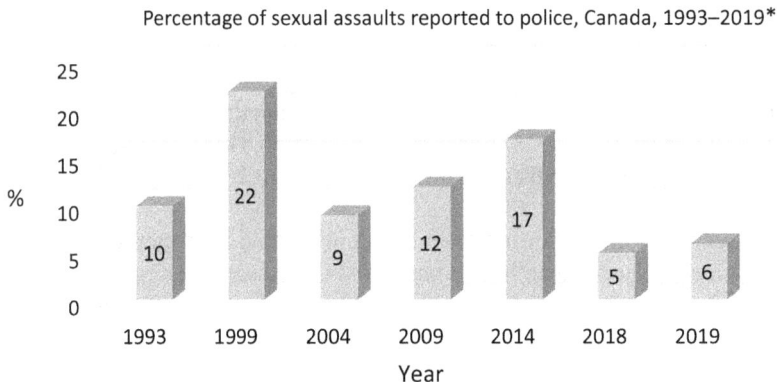

*Canadians aged 15 years and older

Figure 2.3 Percentage of sexual assaults reported to police as indicated in the GSS victimisation cycle survey from 1993 to 2019.

Source: Adapted from Statistics Canada.

even if an accused has not been identified (Canadian Centre for Justice Statistics, 2018; Greenland & Cotter, 2018; Moreau, 2019).

Victimisation surveys have not consistently included data on reasons for not reporting sexual assault. A study by Gartner and Doob (1994) that evaluated trends in criminal victimisation between 1988 and 1993 had a data table of victimisations not reported to the police by reason and incident type (including sexual assault). The table[3] revealed that 50% of the respondents stated that they did not report because they did not want to get involved with the police, that the police could not do anything (28%), or that the police would not help (20%).

A 2014 victimisation study conducted by Perreault (2015) included similar variables to Gartner and Doob's 1993 study and underlying themes regarding views of police resonated the same. Comparable to 1993, 45% of the respondents stated that they did not report because they did not want the hassle of dealing with the police. Additional reasons that are more reflective of biases included that "police would not have considered the incident important enough" (43%), and approximately "13% of respondents claimed they did not report because of unsatisfactory service from police" in the past (Perreault, 2015, p. 41). Reporting to the police presents the risk of being subjected to callous or insensitive treatment and secondary victimisation from the justice system (Johnson et al., 2013). Victims' reluctance to report sexual assault to police is often reinforced by negative and sometimes traumatising experiences described by other victims who have spoken with police or have participated in the CJS (Cotter & Savage, 2019; Venema, 2016).

The most current GSS on crime victimisation was in 2019 and took a different approach by classifying the reasons for not reporting violent victimisation to police by gender rather than by type of offence (Cotter, 2021). Consistent with the other two tables in 1993 and 2014, a top reason for men and women not reporting any violent victimisation did not want the hassle of dealing with police (51% and 44%, respectively). Other notable additions to the 2019 survey are listed in the table with their corresponding percentages (see Table 2.1).

Reasons for not reporting cited by more women than men reflect that women experience much higher rates of sexual assault than men. As illustrated by Table 2.1, the most prominent reason that women chose not to report was due to beliefs that perpetrators would not be held accountable, which is not unwarranted. Between 2009 and 2014, the attrition rate – defined broadly as a reduction of criminal incidents as they are processed through the CJS – was more evident for sexual assault than for physical assault at all levels of the justice system (Rotenberg, 2017b). This means that more incidents reported to police did not proceed to charges, court, or possible convictions (see Figure 2.4).

Table 2.1 GSS questions, by sex, asking Canadians' reasons for not reporting their victimisation to the police.

Reason for not reporting	Women (percent)	Men (percent)
The offender would not be adequately punished.	43	25
Did not think it could be reported.	38	9
Shame or embarrassment.	34	6
Feared/did not want hassle of court process.	33	30
Would not be believed.	25	7

Source: Adapted from Statistics Canada

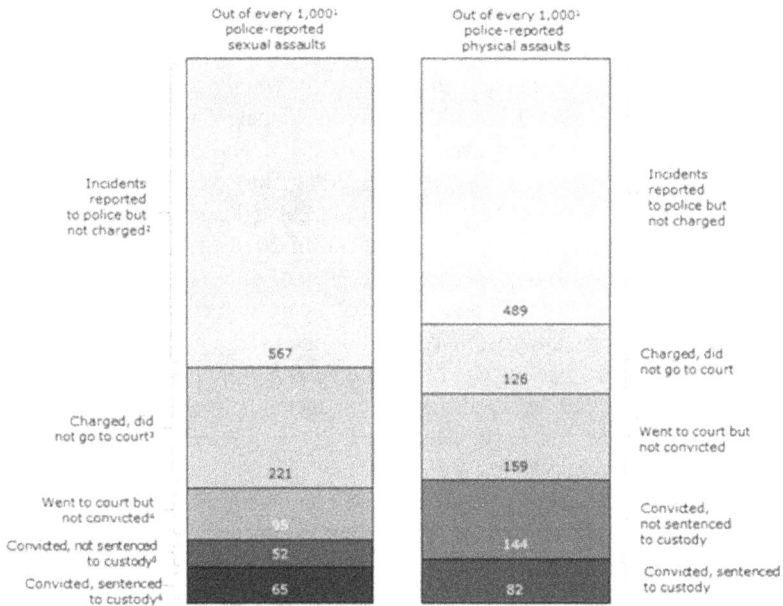

Figure 2.4 Attrition of criminal incidents from police to court, sexual assault versus physical assault, adjusted out of 1,000, Canada, 2009 to 2014.

Source: Rotenberg, C. (2017, October 26). From arrest to conviction: Court outcomes of police-reported sexual assaults in Canada, 2009 to 2014. *Juristat* (Statistics Canada Catalogue no. 85-002-X). https://www150.statcan.gc.ca/n1/pub/85-002-x/2017001/article/54870-eng.htm

Statistics Canada's report on police-reported criminal incidents (Rotenberg, 2017b) confirms that for every five sexual assaults reported by police, one went to court while four did not. And only about one in ten (12%) sexual assaults reported to police led to a criminal conviction, and 7% of those, resulted in a custodial sentence (Rotenberg, 2017b). Negative experiences with the CJS, such as ill-trained police who do not believe complainants, or prosecutors whose over-burdened caseloads do not allow for prosecuting all incidents, can deter reporting. Furthermore, delayed, or lengthy court processes, or unmet expectations about the outcomes of reporting can also deter reporting (Cotter & Savage, 2019; Johnson, 2012).

Disproportionate impact

Sexual assault is under-reported to police and large portion of this crime disproportionately targets some groups more than others (Cotter, 2021).

Gender

SV is understood to be a gendered crime, where women and gender diverse people experience sexual assault at disproportionate rates in comparison to men, a fact that remains persistent across time and jurisdictions (Benoit et al., 2015; Brennan & Taylor-Butts, 2008; Burczycka, 2021; Conroy, 2018; Conroy & Cotter, 2017; Elliott et al., 2004; Kaufman, 2008; Kong et al., 2003; Perreault, 2015; Sinha, 2013). In 2018 in Canada, approximately 4.7 million women (representing 30% of all women 15 years and older) self-reported that they had been sexually assaulted at least once since the age of 15. For comparison, 1.2 million men (8%) had reported being sexually assaulted since the age of 15 (Cotter & Savage, 2019). The statistics derived from victimisation surveys conducted between 1999 and 2019 in Canada show the discrepancy between the rates of sexual assault reported to police and by gender (see Figure 2.5).

For the past 20 years, women have been, on average, almost five times (4.9%) more likely to be targets of sexual assault than men (Besserer & Trainor, 2000; Brennan & Taylor-Butts, 2008; Cotter, 2021; Gannon & Mihorean, 2005; Perreault, 2015; Perreault & Brennan, 2010). Specialised populations are more likely to experience discrimination or unfair treatment (Cotter, 2021), and characteristics such as age, gender identity and expression, race, and mental or physical disabilities can increase the risk of SV (Beauchamp, 2008; Boyce, 2016; Burczycka, 2018; Conroy, 2018; Conroy & Cotter, 2017; Cotter, 2018, 2021; Cotter & Beaupré, 2014; Cotter & Savage, 2019; Ibrahim, 2018; Jaffray, 2020; Perreault, 2015; Rotenberg, 2017a; Rotenberg, 2019; Rothman et al., 2011; Simpson, 2018). Although any gender can experience violence in Canada, SV is disproportionally experienced by individuals who identify as female, gender diverse, or as a sexual minority (often referred to as 2SLGBTQIA+).

Sexual assault (levels 1, 2, and 3) self-reported rate, sex,
Canada, 1999–2019

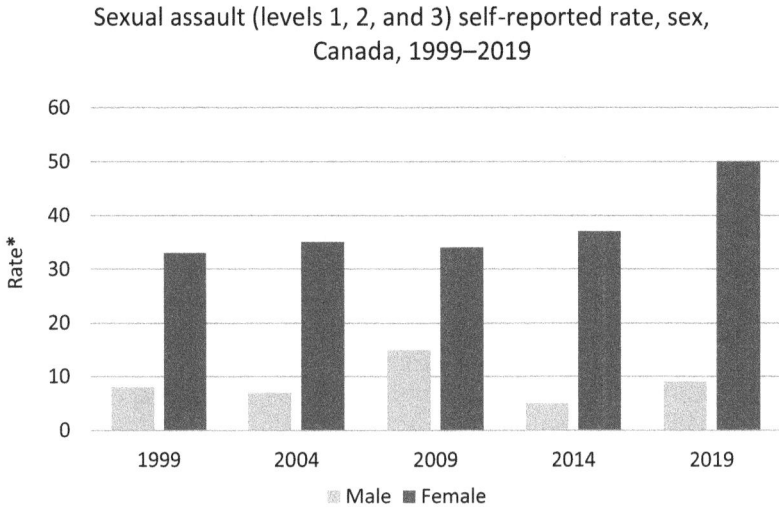

*Rate per 1,000 population 15 years of age or older

Figure 2.5 Self-reported rates of sexual assaults, by sex, from 1999 to 2019.
Source: Adapted from Statistics Canada.

Sexuality identity

Research on SV against gender diverse people is a comparatively new area
of study. In 2014, victimisation surveys began to incorporate information on
sexual orientation, which revealed significantly higher rates of sexual assault
against individuals who self-identify as lesbian, gay, or bisexual (Beauchamp,
2008; Conroy & Cotter, 2017; Cotter, 2018, 2021; Jaffray, 2020; Perreault,
2015; Rothman et al., 2011; Simpson, 2018). In 2018, a *Survey of Safety in
Public and Private Spaces* (SSPPS) was conducted to advance knowledge
of GBV in Canada (Jaffray, 2020) resulting in an estimated that one million
Canadians are sexual minorities (the term used in the study), representing
4% of the population aged 15 years and older (Jaffray, 2020). And excluding
violence committed by an intimate partner, 59% of sexual minorities reported
that they had been physically or sexually assaulted since age 15, compared to
37% reported by heterosexual Canadians in the study (Jaffray, 2020).

Individuals who identify as lesbian, gay, bisexual, or trans are at an
increased risk of being targeted (Conroy & Cotter, 2017; Cotter & Savage,
2019; Perreault, 2015; Rothman et al., 2011; Simpson, 2018). One study by

Cotter (2021) revealed that bisexual Canadians experienced victimisation rates over nine times higher than their heterosexual counterparts, consistent with the 2014 victimisation survey results (Simpson, 2018). Bisexual women and bisexual men experience sexual assault at comparable rates (63% and 58%, respectively). Notably, bisexual women are almost four times more likely than heterosexual women to be victims of sexual assault (11% vs. 3%) (Cotter & Savage, 2019).

In Canada, research on the experiences of trans people is still in its infancy. Much of the existing research on trans people and the issues that affect them can be distinct from their sexual orientation (Jaffray, 2020; James et al., 2016). The 2019 SSPPS revealed that approximately 75,000 Canadians identify as trans (representing 0.24% of the Canadian population aged 15 and older) and are over-represented among those who experience sexual assault or unwanted sexualised behaviours (Griner et al., 2017; Jaffray, 2020; Mitchell et al., 2014).

Disabilities

Canadians who self-identified as asexual/gender diverse, and who have a disability, were more likely to report that they had been sexually assaulted (46%) since age 15 than those who did not have a disability (29%) (Jaffray, 2020). Research has shown that individuals with disabilities – including sensory, physical, cognitive, mental health-related, or any other unspecified disability, are at a higher risk of SV, which may be partially attributed to greater vulnerability, negative social attitudes and perceptions, and abuses of trust (Benedet & Grant, 2014; Conroy & Cotter, 2017; Luce et al., 2010; Meer & Combrinck, 2015; Nosek et al., 2001). The rate of sexual assault among individuals with any disability was approximately two times higher than those without a disability (Conroy & Cotter, 2017), and individuals with mental health-related disabilities are five times more likely to experience SV than those without such a disability (Conroy & Cotter, 2017). The over-representation of persons with disabilities among victims of violent crimes is more notable for women. In 2019, the rates of sexual assault were over four times higher for women with a disability compared to women without a disability and about 14 times more likely than men without a disability (Cotter, 2021).

Indigenous (First Nations, Métis, or Inuit) persons with a disability were more likely than non-Indigenous persons with a disability to have been violently victimised (Cotter, 2018). Nearly three-quarters (72%) of Indigenous people with physical, cognitive, or mental health disabilities have experienced at least one sexual assault since the age of 15, compared with 52% of Indigenous people without disabilities and 54% of non-Indigenous people with disabilities (Perreault, 2022). Overall, the rates of victimisation in Canada have been historically higher for Indigenous people (Boyce, 2016; Conroy & Cotter, 2017; Dylan et al., 2008; Gannon & Mihorean, 2005; Perreault, 2015, 2022; Perreault & Brennan, 2010; Simpson, 2018). The GSS on victimisation for 2009, 2014, and 2019 illustrate that the rates of self-reported sexual assault for Indigenous persons are proportionately higher than for those who are non-Indigenous (see Figure 2.6) (Boyce, 2016; Conroy & Cotter, 2017; Cotter, 2021; Perreault & Brennan, 2010).

The rate of sexual assault against Indigenous peoples was approximately three times higher than that among non-Indigenous people in 2009 and 2014 (Conroy & Cotter, 2017; Perreault & Brennan, 2010). A study by Cotter (2021) revealed that after controlling for other characteristics such as age, gender, and childhood maltreatment, it was determined that Indigenous identities alone were not associated with a greater likelihood of violent victimisation, which could explain the mischaracterisation of self-reported rates of sexual assault for that year. But when considering those variables, there was a disproportionate risk of violent victimisation.

Other statistics from 2018 to 2020 show that nearly two-thirds (62%) of Indigenous peoples had experienced at least one sexual or physical assault since the age of 15, compared to 42% of non-Indigenous peoples (Statistics Canada, 2022). Violent victimisation rates are exceptionally high among

Self-reported rates of sexual assault, Indigenous* and non-Indigenous respondents, 2009, 2014, and 2019

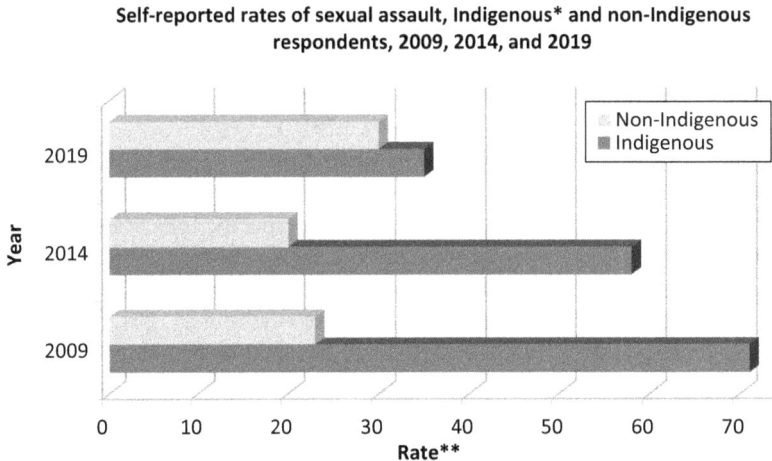

*Includes those who identified as First Nations, Métis or Inuit.
**Rate is calculated per 1,000 population aged 15 years and older

Figure 2.6 Self-reported rates of sexual assault comparing Indigenous and non-Indigenous respondents, 2009, 2014, and 2019.

Source: Adapted from Statistics Canada.

Indigenous females (Conroy, 2018; Cotter, 2018; Hotton Mahony et al., 2017; Hutchins, 2013; Perreault, 2015; Simpson, 2018), with almost half (46%) of them experiencing sexual assault in their lifetime compared to about a third (33%) of non-Indigenous women (Heidinger, 2022). Indigenous peoples who self-identified as gender diverse also experienced a higher prevalence of violent victimisation since age 15, with 65% reporting they had been sexually assaulted compared with 37% of their non-Indigenous and non-gender diverse counterparts (Jaffray, 2020).

SV at PSIs

Decades of research on the prevalence of SV in Canada have consistently found that people aged 18–25 experience SV and other forms of GBV in higher proportions than other demographics (Burczycka, 2020; Conroy & Cotter, 2017; Perreault, 2015; Rotenberg, 2017a). Increased attention has been given to sexual assault on campuses (Canadian Federation of Students, n.d.; Conroy & Cotter, 2017; Metropolitan Action Committee on Violence Against Women, 2016; Weikle, 2016), which prompted a study conducted by Statistics Canada in 2019 that evaluated the characteristics, prevalence, and impacts of sexual assault at Canadian PSIs. The study indicated that approximately 2.5 million students were attending PSIs, and of that population, 11% of female students and 4% of male students experienced a sexual assault the previous year. That equates to roughly 110,000 and 60,000 students, respectively (Statistics Canada, 2020). Other surveys have revealed that 20–25% of students reported having experienced a sexual assault in a post-secondary setting (Lee, 2020; SVPC, 2017).

The prevalence of SV is elevated in the first years of post-secondary education, where 90% of sexual assaults are committed against women (Conroy & Cotter, 2017; Statistics Canada, 2020). A specific time of heightened campus-related SV – referred to as the *red zone*[4] – occurs during the first eight weeks of classes. Statistics show that more than 50% of campus sexual assaults (CSAs) take place during this time (Bourassa et al., 2017; Colpitts, 2019; Cranney, 2015; EVABC, 2016; Flack et al., 2008; Kimble et al., 2008; Martell Consulting Services Ltd., 2014). Most sexual assaults are perpetrated by peers, specifically by students who are male (Burczycka, 2020, 2021; Statistics Canada, 2020). In 2019, students reported that men perpetrated more than seven in ten (73%) sexual assaults (Burczycka, 2020). Some studies reveal that CSAs are often committed by serial perpetrators (60%), each averaging between five and six assaults (Lisak & Miller, 2002; Quinlan, 2017) and can include coercion, manipulation, and incapacity to consent (Burczycka, 2020). One in six (16%) women indicated that at least one sexual assault had happened because of continuous verbal pressure, even after saying "no" or being unable to consent because they were intoxicated (Burczycka, 2020).

Campus culture can reflect the attitudes of the greater community, and students living with visible or invisible disabilities, students who identify as gender diverse, and students who are Indigenous can experience exclusion and discrimination caused by unequal power relationships. These populations are often under-represented at PSIs but over-represented in statistics of sexual assault in post-secondary settings (Bourassa et al., 2017; Burczycka, 2020). Students living with some form of disability – particularly women with mental disabilities – experienced over twice the proportion of sexual assaults compared to students without a disability (12% vs. 5%) (Burczycka, 2020; Conroy & Cotter, 2017). For sexual minorities, sexual assault was twice as common among bisexual students (16%) as among heterosexual students (7%) (Burczycka, 2020; Coulter & Rankin, 2020), and about one in six (18%) trans students were sexually assaulted during their time attending post-secondary school (Burczycka, 2020; Coulter & Rankin, 2020; de Heer & Jones, 2017; Perez & Hussey, 2014).

In recent years, campus culture has been criticised for fostering colonial violence through trivialising Indigenous identities and experiences (Bourassa et al., 2017) and sustaining rape culture. Overall, the rates of SV against Indigenous people, especially Indigenous women, are disproportionally higher than among those who identify as non-Indigenous (Conroy & Cotter, 2017). In contrast to the general population, a 2019 study by Burczycka (2020) revealed that Indigenous women had a similar prevalence of sexual assault in a Canadian post-secondary setting to non-Indigenous women (10% and 11%). And notably, Indigenous men in post-secondary experienced a prevalence that was more than double that of their non-Indigenous counterparts (9% vs. 4%).

Identifying the prevalence of SV among students and specialised populations is valuable and informative, but it is imperative to acknowledge that multiple intersections of characteristics and social locations can compound victimisation risk (Armstrong et al., 2018; Cotter & Savage, 2019; Shankar & Tavcer, 2021). Intersectionality recognises that individuals are impacted differently by varied characteristics and social locations (e.g., class, gender, race, sexuality, disability, and citizenship) that shape their standing in society (Crenshaw, 1989, 1991). Intersectionality relates to systems and structures of oppression and highlights how power is unevenly distributed (Almeida et al., 2019; Colpitts, 2019; Hill Collins & Bilge, 2016).

An intersectional approach provides a unique perspective that helps us understand how different identities are targeted and impacted by SV. It challenges the belief that SV is an interpersonal issue and amplifies it as a societal issue (Colpitts, 2019). An intersectional approach can be used as a tool for analysis, advocacy, and policy development (Khosla & Barth, 2008). Without it, researchers will continue to approach SV with the danger of a single narrative (Harris & Linder, 2017; Nelson, 2017).

What sustains SV

SV does not discriminate and can happen to anyone, despite their gender, age, race, social, economic status, or sexual identity (Conroy, 2018; Cotter & Savage, 2019; Statistics Canada, 2016). However, police-reported and self-reported statistics confirm that certain groups are disproportionally impacted, and the intersection of those vulnerabilities increases risk of being targeted. SV is informed by racism, sexism, classism, ableism, and colonialism and is sustained by systemic power, privilege, and existing systems of oppression (Almeida et al., 2019; Benoit et al., 2015; Colpitts, 2019).

Racialised persons

Racialised persons disproportionally experience SV, and its prevalence cannot be fully understood without understanding how it relates to colonialism (Benoit et al., 2015; SVPC, 2017). Research has linked the violent victimisation of Indigenous people in Canada to past and present colonial policies (SVPC, 2017; Statistics Canada, 2022). Colonialist practices under the *Indian Act*,[5] residential and day schools,[6] the forced removal of Indigenous children from their families (i.e., the Sixties Scoop[7] during the 1950s–1980s, which some argue continues today through provincial child welfare agencies), and other policies that have resulted in the loss of culture, identity, and family structures (Benoit et al., 2015; Brownridge, 2008; Spiwak & Brownridge, 2005; SVPC, 2017). The colonial system is rooted in a lack of consent and oppressive and exploitative relationships (Colpitts, 2019).

Researchers note that Indigenous women remain the most victimised group in Canada (Nelson, 2017; Ontario Native Women's Association, 2011). A case in point is the way Indigenous women are disproportionately impacted by SV because of intergenerational trauma, patriarchal laws denying equality, and systemic racism that continues to diminish the lived experiences of the entire population (Benoit et al., 2015; Brownridge, 2008; Spiwak & Brownridge, 2005; Trainor & Mihorean, 2001). Indigenous women's over-representation in victimisation illustrates how intersections of racism, colonialism, and patriarchy can compound experiences of violence (Colpitts, 2019; Deer, 2015; Simpson, 2018).

Patriarchy

Patriarchal discourse and ideology have influenced cultural, social, and gender norms, inevitably creating and sustaining a society of inequality (Almeida et al., 2019; Benoit et al., 2015; Beres, 2020; SVPC, 2017). Feminist analysis asserts that sexualised violence exists because of power imbalances rooted in patriarchy (Avalon Sexual Assault Centre, 2015). Patriarchal society facilitates white male's authority, privilege, and power over others (particularly women and racialised people), leading to an increased risk of exploitation and violence (Benoit et al., 2015; Colpitts, 2019; Johnson et al., 2013; SVPC, 2017). Women and racialised people are viewed as inferior and valued less, and crimes explicitly committed against them are rarely considered violations of human rights (Cusmano, 2018). Patriarchal ideology is one of domination and control and forms the basis of rape culture within society (Cusmano, 2018; SVPC, 2017).

Rape culture

Rape culture is complex and about far more than rape and culture; it is a form of structural violence rooted in patriarchal societies that normalises systemic misogyny (Cusmano, 2018). Rape culture is a sociological concept in which dominant ideas, social practices, and societal institutions implicitly or explicitly condone sexual aggression of men and violence against women (Bourassa et al., 2017; Buchwald et al., 1993; Cusmano, 2018; Samples, 2015; Skrypnek, 2021; VanTassel, 2020). The term's origin can be traced to the 1970s, when second-wave feminists in the USA wanted to bring attention to prevailing norms and attitudes that justify, tolerate, and minimise rape (Bourassa et al., 2017; Garcia & Vemuri, 2017). As illustrated, rape culture is informed by sexism, racism, colonialism, patriarchy, and toxic masculinity (Colpitts, 2019). It reflects how a society collectively tolerates, excuses, and even encourages SV (Ridgeway, 2014).

Accepting that rape culture exists is tricky because it is somehow refuted and widely accepted simultaneously. As rape culture is nuanced, to see it *in action* may not be overt each time. The subtleties of rape culture can best be exemplified through sexual objectification; a Canadian study by Cotter and Savage (2019) revealed that more than 3.8 million women (25% of those 15 years of age and older) stated that they had experienced unwanted sexual attention in public (e.g., comments, gestures, body language, whistles, or catcalls), in the past 12 months. Some other examples of rape culture include the following:

• Rape jokes and those who defend them.
• Trivialising violence committed by boys and men by excusing their behaviour with the phrase "boys will be boys."

- Slut shaming and victim blaming.
- Pro-rape fraternity chants.
- The belief that women allow themselves to be raped.

This list is far from exhaustive but illustrates the extent of this deeply ingrained societal issue. The consequences of rape culture are reflected in *rape myths*, which are beliefs that contribute to victim blaming, shaming, perpetrator absolution, and the rationalisation that rape is inevitable (Cusmano, 2018; Edwards et al., 2011; MacKinnon, 2001; SVPC, 2017). Rape culture fails to protect victims of SV, and rape myths shift the blame away from perpetrators (i.e., women often bear the responsibility and accountability for sexual assaults rather than their attacker) (Cusmano, 2018).

Rape myths

Rape mythology was first acknowledged in the 1970s (Grubb & Turner, 2012), and advocates have long worked to debunk these societal assumptions. Rape myths are shaped by sexism and prevail because they contribute to false beliefs that discredit the reality of SV and those who experience it (Burt, 1980; Lonsway & Fitzgerald, 1994; McMahon & Farmer, 2011). Common ideologies surrounding rape myths include *It wasn't really rape*; *He didn't mean to do it*; *She wanted it*; *She asked for it*; or *She lied* (Deming et al., 2013; Hildebrand & Najdowski, 2015; Payne et al., 1999). They are labelled as "myths" because they are not based on facts but are socially constructed and reflect imbalances of power (SVPC, 2017).

Most rape myths are rooted in *victim blaming*, which occurs when individuals who have experienced SV are treated with suspicion, accused of lying, or blamed for their victimisation (Cusmano, 2018; MacKinnon, 2001). Research shows that one in five victims of sexual assault felt blamed for their victimisation and identified two principal sources of blame: The perpetrator and friends or family (Cotter & Savage, 2019). Common themes of victim blaming include questioning the person's choice of clothing, if they consumed drugs and/or alcohol, behaviour believed to have provoked the assault, and so on (Deming et al., 2013). See Table 2.2 for a few popularly held rape myths and their corresponding facts.

Researchers of rape mythology believe that adherence to rape myths is culturally widespread (Burt, 1980; Deming et al., 2013; Johnson et al., 1997; Payne et al., 1999), and many individuals may find themselves subconsciously adhering to myths. In a study by Edwards et al. (2011), male and female respondents (25% and 30%, respectively) agreed with most rape myths; however, males were more likely to endorse these myths. As males are more often the perpetrators of SV, it would make sense that they more often endorse rape myths than females, who are more likely victimised.

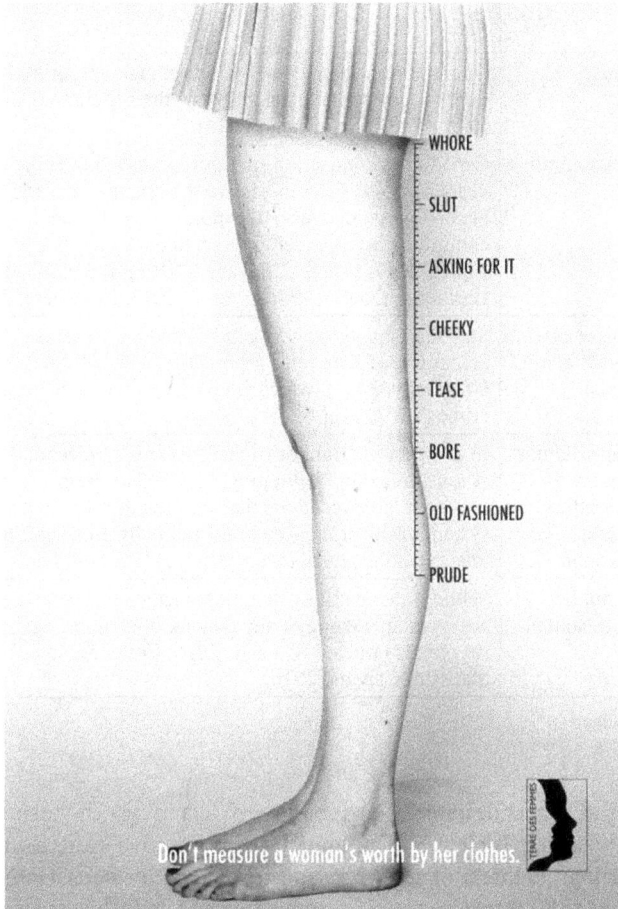

Figure 2.7 Campaign poster challenging the rape myth that clothing equates to violence.

Source: Theresa Wlokka and Frida Regenheim for Terres des Femmes. This student campaign titled "A woman's worth" was published in Germany in June 2014. It was created for the brand: Terre Des Femmes, by ad school: Miami Ad School.

Rape culture maintains the fallacy that rape is inevitable and that women are responsible for taking precautions to prevent getting raped (Filipovic, 2008). Suggestions such as going out with a friend, taking a self-defence class, avoiding dark alleys, and being alone at night perpetrate the *stranger-danger* myth (beliefs that strangers perpetrate sexual assaults), which

Table 2.2 Some common rape myths and the facts that dispute them.

Myth	Fact
SV is rare.	One in three women and one in six men in Canada have experienced some forms of SV in their lifetime (Conroy & Cotter, 2017; Senn et al., 2014).
Strangers commit SV.	Canadian victimisation surveys conducted over the past 30 years have consistently shown that the majority (55–80%, depending on the year) of reported sexual assaults were committed by offenders known to the victim (Conroy & Cotter, 2017; Cotter & Savage, 2019; Filipovic, 2008; Gartner & Doob, 1994; Johnson, 2012; Rotenberg, 2017a).
People lie or give false reports about being sexually assaulted.	Statistics show that between 2% and 8% of sexual assaults across Canada are false reports (Lisak et al., 2010; McGill University, 2015), which is consistent with other reported crimes such as robbery.
If someone did not scream or try to fight their attacker off, it was not sexual assault.	In addition to "fight or flight" responses to fear and stress, "freezing," "flopping," or "befriending" are other uncontrollable reactions that are governed by the limbic system of the brain. The brain and body do what it needs to survive the attack (Marx et al., 2008).
Men cannot be sexually assaulted.	While statistics show that most victims of sexual assault are women, anyone of any gender, orientation, sex, race, or religion is targeted (Conroy, 2018; Cotter & Savage, 2019; Statistics Canada, 2016).

Source: Authors.

continues to persist despite various sources of data irrevocably demonstrating otherwise (see Table 2.2). The stranger-rape narrative instils a culture of fear by using the threat of sexual assault to keep women constantly afraid (Filipovic, 2008). It places the onus on women and shifts blame away from those perpetrating the violence. For example, if a stranger rapes a woman, her decisions are called into question (e.g., Why was she walking home alone at night? Why did she drink so much?), and if a woman is raped by someone known to her, her actions and underlying motives are scrutinised (e.g., Why did she go to that house party? Was it rape or just a morning after regret?) (Filipovic, 2008). Interestingly, women who were sexually assaulted by a friend or acquaintance were three times more likely to have felt blamed for their victimisation than those who were assaulted by a stranger (31% vs. 10%) (Cotter & Savage, 2019).

Some rape myths assert that women will claim they were raped after they regret having a consensual sexual activity or because they are seeking revenge (Cotter, 2021). Yet, the rates of false allegations are low and consistent with other reported crimes such as robbery (see Table 2.8). There is no evidence that victims of sexual assault are any more likely than victims of other crimes, such as theft or robbery, to make false reports to police. International research on false reporting indicates that it happens between 2% and 8% of cases (Greenland & Cotter, 2018; Johnson, 2012; Lonsway et al., 2009; Venema, 2016). Research suggests that preconceived notions about sexual victimisation (i.e., the myth of a perfect victim) can harm victims when their lived experiences do not match what the person would define as a sexual assault. Victims whose sexual assaults do not meet these unachievable standards are less likely to report their experiences due to fear of not being believed and secondary victimisation (Cotter & Savage, 2019; Harber et al., 2015; Johnson, 2012). And these "ideologies are so pervasive that they also factor into the discretionary decisions made by police or prosecutors and as such have an enormous impact on conviction rates and prosecution of cases" (Grubb & Turner, 2012, p. 445).

Rape culture and rape myths are entangled within the CJS. Despite the reforms made to the *Criminal Code* aimed at ensuring equality, discriminatory stereotypes and existing stigmas still influence the perspectives and behaviours of police officers, lawyers, judges, and subsequent decisions made by the courts (Craig, 2018; McMahon & Farmer, 2011; SVPC, 2017). Common assumptions about sexual assault include when a woman says no (at least initially), she means yes or how a victim dresses or their behaviour prior to the assault is, at least in part, to blame for the assault (Hildebrand & Najdowski, 2015). This is evident in a study of Canadian judicial rulings (Craig, 2018), which illustrated that judges invoke victim-blaming language and frequently describe sexual assaults as erotic, romantic, or affectionate acts (Craig, 2018; Coates & Wade, 2004; Shaffer, 2012). Prevailing sexist ideologies and dominant patriarchal influences in the legal system create barriers and represent significant challenges that permeate the reporting, investigating, prosecuting, and adjudicating of sexual assault cases (CICS, 2018; SVPC, 2017). And whether subtle or blatant, rape culture within the CJS ultimately prevents the law from protecting victims (Shaffer, 2012).

Conclusion

SV is a provocative topic. And measuring how it is understood is complex because those who experience (and perpetrate) it may not be cognisant of the underlying social structures and systems that produce and reproduce it (Cotter & Savage, 2019). SV is preventable, not inevitable. It is both an individual experience and a confluence of structural forces (Quinlan, 2017), and its impacts are significant and long lasting. The prevalence of SV in

Canada has stagnated for the last 30+ years and will remain that way unless its significant issues are addressed. This chapter unpacked SV in Canada and evaluated the contributors to its prevalence. It highlighted the concept of intersectionality and the importance of incorporating an intersectional approach. Without it, analysis, advocacy, and policy development will continue using a single narrative that will further marginalise populations that experience high proportions of SV. This chapter emphasises the complexities of rape culture and rape myths and their causal relationship to structural and SV. What remains is a call to dismantle rape culture and address the structural and systemic nature of SV.

Notes

1 Such as the patriarchal construct of promiscuity dictates that a promiscuous woman is less virtuous, less a victim, and less likely to be believed should she claim sexual assault.
2 The General Social Survey (GSS) is administered through Statistics Canada. Established in 1985, it is a series of independent, voluntary, cross-sectional surveys, each covering one topic in-depth. Although administered annually, the topic of focus changes each year. The GSS for victimisation is on a five-year cycle the most recent data collected in 2019. The GSS on victimisation asks Canadians about reported and unreported victimisation, including experiences of crime, violence, and abuse by current or past spouse or partner; the use of services available to help victims of abuse or crime; fear of crime; crime prevention; and social disorder and experiences of discrimination.
3 See Table 8 in (Gartner & Dobb, 1994).
4 The Red Zone is described as a time of heightened instances of sexual assault that happens during the first eight weeks of university or college where more than 50% of all campus sexual assaults are reported to have occurred.
5 The *Indian Act* came into power in 1876 and is a consolidation of several colonial laws that sought to subjugate and assimilate Indigenous peoples into European-White culture imposed within Canada.
6 Residential and day schools were established as early as the 1600s by the Catholic church and by 1883, these schools began to receive funding from the federal government, which then permitted the RCMP to take children from their families and force them into those schools. The last school closed in 1996.
7 The "Sixties Scoop" refers to a government-sanctioned forced removal or "scooping" of Indigenous children from their families from the 1960s well into the 1980s, and their subsequent adoption into predominantly non-Indigenous, middle-class families across the United States and Canada.

References

Aghtaie, N., & Ganjoli, G. (2015). Chapter one: Key issues researching gender-based violence. In N. Aghtaie & G. Ganjoli (Eds.), *Understanding gender-based violence: National and international contexts* (pp. 3–17). Routledge.

Almeida, R. V., Werkmeister-Rozas, L. M., Cross-Denny, B., Lee, K. K., & Yamada, A.M. (2019). Coloniality and intersectionality in social work education and practice. *Journal of Progressive Human Services*, *30*(2), 148–164. https://doi.org/10. 1080/10428232.2019.1574195

Armstrong, E. A., Gleckman-Krut, M., & Johnson, L. (2018). Silence, power, and inequality: An intersectional approach to sexual violence. *Annual Review of Sociology*, *44*(1). https://doi.org/10.1146/annurev-soc-073117-041410

Avalon Sexual Assault Centre. (2015). *Feminist gender based analysis and approach to preventing sexualized violence/abuse*. https://avaloncentre.ca/policies/

Basile, K., Smith, S., Breiding, M., Black, M., & Mahendra, R. (2014). *Sexual violence surveillance: Uniform definitions and recommended data elements*. www. cdc.gov/violenceprevention/pdf/sv_surveillance_definitionsl-2009-a.pdf

Beauchamp, D. (2008, February 28). Sexual orientation and victimisation, 2004. *Canadian Centre for Justice Statistics Profile Series*. (Statistics Canada Catalogue no. 85F0033M, no. 16). https://www150.statcan.gc.ca/n1/en/pub/85f0033m/85f 0033m2008016-eng.pdf?st=LZIFkJ8W

Benedet, J., & Grant, I. (2014). Sexual assault and the meaning of power and authority for women with mental disabilities. *Feminist Legal Studies*, *22*(2), 131–154. www.proquest.com/docview/1553293869/fulltextPDF/1A03AB525B6D4C71P Q/1?accountid=8056

Benoit, C., Shumka, L., Phillips, R., Kennedy, M. C., & Belle-Isle, L. (2015, December). Issue brief: Sexual violence against women in Canada. *For the Status of Women Canada*. https://cfc-swc.gc.ca/svawc-vcsfc/index-en.html

Beres, M. (2020). Perspectives of rape-prevention educators on the role of consent in sexual violence prevention. *Sex Education*, *20*(2), 227–238. https://doi.org/10. 1080/14681811.2019.1621744

Besserer, S., & Trainor, C. (2000, November 2). Criminal victimisation in Canada, 1999. *Juristat 20*(10) (Statistics Canada Catalogue no. 85–002-XIE). https:// www150.statcan.gc.ca/n1/pub/85-002-x/85-002-x2000010-eng.pdf

Biesenthal, L. (1991, June). Sexual assault legislation in Canada: An evaluation. *Justice Research Notes*, No. 3. The Department of Justice Canada. www.ojp.gov/ pdffiles1/Digitization/140416NCJRS.pdf

Bourassa, C., Bendig, M., Oleson, E. J., Ozog, C. A., Billan, J. L., Owl, N., & Ross-Hopley, L. (2017). Campus violence, Indigenous women, and the policy void. In E. Quinlan, A. Quinlan, C. Fogel, & G. Taylor (Eds.), *Sexual violence at Canadian universities: Activism, institutional responses, and strategies for change* (pp. 45–59). ProQuest Ebook Central. https://ebookcentral.proquest.com

Boyce, J. (2016, June 28). Victimisation of aboriginal people in Canada, 2014. *Juristat (36)*1 (Statistics Canada Catalogue no. 85–002-X). https://www150.statcan. gc.ca/n1/pub/85-002-x/2016001/article/14631-eng.htm

Brennan, S., & Taylor-Butts, A. (2008, December). *Sexual assault in Canada, 2004 and 2007*. Canadian Centre for Justice Statistics. Profile Series. No. 19. (Statistics Canada Catalogue no. 85F0033M). https://www150.statcan.gc.ca/n1/en/ pub/85f0033m/85f0033m2008019-eng.pdf?st=rxS14fst

Brownridge, D. (2008). Understanding the elevated risk of partner violence against Aboriginal women: A comparison of two nationally representative surveys of

Canada. *Journal of Family Violence*, *23*(5), 353–367. https://doi.org/10.1007/s10896-008-9160-0

Buchwald, E., Fletcher, P. O., & Roth, M. (1993). *Transforming a rape culture*. Milkweed Editions.

Burczycka, M. (2018, December 5). Police-reported intimate partner violence in Canada, 2017: In Family violence in Canada: A statistical profile, 2017. *Juristat* (Statistics Canada Catalogue no. 85–002-X). https://www150.statcan.gc.ca/n1/pub/85-002-x/2018001/article/54978/02-eng.htm

Burczycka, M. (2020, September 14). Students' experiences of unwanted sexualized behaviours and sexual assault at postsecondary schools in the Canadian provinces, 2019. *Juristat* (Statistics Canada Catalogue no. 85–002-X). https://www150.statcan.gc.ca/n1/en/pub/85-002-x/2020001/article/00005-eng.pdf?st=SyK5goe_

Burczycka, M. (2021, August 12). Workers' experiences of inappropriate sexualized behaviours, sexual assault and gender-based discrimination in the Canadian provinces, 2020. *Juristat* (Statistics Canada Catalogue no. 85–002-X). https://www150.statcan.gc.ca/n1/en/pub/85-002-x/2021001/article/00015-eng.pdf?st=6I3YlaLy

Burt, M. R. (1980). Cultural myths and supports for rape. *Journal of Personality and Social Psychology*, *38*(2), 217–230. https://doi.org/10.1037/0022-3514.38.2.217

Buss, D., Majury, D., Moore, D., Rigakos, G. S., & Singh, R. (2016, June). *The response to sexual violence at Ontario university campuses: Final report*. www.academia.edu/32063786/The_Response_to_Sexual_Violence_at_Ontario_University_Campuses

Canadian Association of Chiefs of Police. (2017, February 10). *Canadian framework for collaborative police response on sexual violence*. www.cacp.ca/crime-prevention-committee.html?asst_id=2059

Canadian Centre for Justice Statistics. (2018, July 12). Revising the classification of founded and unfounded criminal incidents in the Uniform Crime Reporting Survey. *Juristat* (Statistics Canada Catalogue no. 85-002-X). https://www150.statcan.gc.ca/n1/pub/85-002-x/2018001/article/54973-eng.htm

Canadian Federation of Students. (n.d.). *A national vision for consent culture in post-secondary education*. www.sfcccanada.org/

Canadian Intergovernmental Conference Secretariat (CICS). (2018). *Reporting, investigating and prosecuting sexual assaults committed against adults: Challenges and promising practices in enhancing access to justice for victims – CICS/SCIC*. https://scics.ca/en/product-produit/reporting-investigating-and-prosecuting-sexual-assaults-committed-against-adults-challenges-and-promising-practices-in-enhancing-access-to-justice-for-victims/#fn23-rf

Cantalupo, N. C. (2016). Title IX civil rights approach and the criminal justice system; enabling separate but coordinate parallel proceedings. In S. C. Wooten & R. W. Mitchell (Eds.), *The crisis of campus sexual violence: critical perspectives on prevention and response* (pp. 125–146). Routledge.

Coates, L., & Wade, A. (2004). Telling it like it isn't: Obscuring perpetrator responsibility for violent crime. *Discourse & Society*, *15*(5), 499–526. https://yorkspace.library.yorku.ca/xmlui/handle/10315/36778

Colpitts, E. M. (2019). *An intersectional analysis of sexual violence policies, responses, and prevention efforts at Ontario universities* (Dissertation). https://

yorkspace.library.yorku.ca/xmlui/bitstream/handle/10315/36778/Colpitts_
Emily_M_2019_PhD.pdf?sequence=2&isAllowed=y

Conroy, S. (2018, December 17). Police-reported violence against girls and young
women in Canada, 2017. *Juristat* (Statistics Canada Catalogue no. 85–002-X).
https://www150.statcan.gc.ca/n1/pub/85-002-x/2018001/article/54981-eng.htm

Conroy, S. (2021, March 2). Family violence in Canada: A statistical profile, 2019.
Juristat (Statistics Canada Catalogue no. 85–002-X). https://www150.statcan.
gc.ca/n1/en/pub/85-002-x/2021001/article/00014-eng.pdf?st=j_yLxP5q

Conroy, S., & Cotter, A. (2017). Self-reported sexual assault in Canada, 2014. *Juristat* (Statistics Canada Catalogue no. 85–002-X). https://www150.statcan.gc.ca/
n1/en/pub/85-002-x/2017001/article/14842-eng.pdf?st=9A3jjLTw

Cook, S. L., Cortina, L. M., & Koss, M. P. (2018, February 7). What's the difference
between sexual abuse, sexual assault, sexual harassment and rape? *The Conversation*. https://theconversation.com/whats-the-difference-between-sexual-abuse-
sexual-assault-sexual-harassment-and-rape-88218

Cotter, A. (2018, March 15). Violent victimisation of women with disabilities, 2014.
Juristat (Statistics Canada Catalogue no. 85–002-X). https://www150.statcan.
gc.ca/n1/pub/85-002-x/2018001/article/54910-eng.htm

Cotter, A. (2021, August 25). Criminal victimisation in Canada, 2019. *Juristat*
(Statistics Canada Catalogue no. 85–002-X). https://www150.statcan.gc.ca/n1/
pub/85-002-x/2021001/article/00014-eng.htm

Cotter, A., & Beaupré, P. (2014, May 28). Police-reported sexual offences against children and youth in Canada, 2012. *Juristat* (Statistics Canada Catalogue no. 85–002-
X). https://www150.statcan.gc.ca/n1/pub/85-002-x/2014001/article/14008-eng.htm

Cotter, A., & Savage, L. (2019, December 5). Gender-based violence and unwanted
sexual behaviour in Canada, 2018: Initial findings from the Survey of Safety in
Public and Private Spaces. *Juristat* (Statistics Canada Catalogue no. 85–002-X).
https://www150.statcan.gc.ca/n1/pub/85-002-x/2019001/article/00017-eng.htm

Coulter, R. W., & Rankin, S. R. (2020). College sexual assault and campus climate
for sexual- and gender-minority undergraduate students. *Journal of Interpersonal
Violence*, *35*(5–6), 1351–1366. https://doi.org/10.1177/0886260517696870

Craig, E. (2016, March 30). Section 276 misconstrued: The failure to properly
interpret and apply Canada's rape shield provisions. *94 Canadian Bar Review*, *1*.
https://ssrn.com/abstract=2756510

Craig, E. (2018). *Putting trials on trial: Sexual assault and the failure of the legal
profession*. McGill-Queen's University Press.

Cranney, S. (2015). The relationship between sexual victimization and year in school
in U.S. colleges: Investigating the parameters of the "red zone". *Journal of Interpersonal Violence*, *30*(17), 3133–3145. https://doi.org/10.1177/0886260514554425

Crenshaw, K. (1989). Demarginalizing the intersection of race and sex: A black feminist critique of antidiscrimination doctrine, feminist theory and antiracist politics.
University of Chicago Legal Forum, *1989*(8), 139–167. https://chicagounbound.
uchicago.edu/uclf/vol1989/iss1/8

Crenshaw, K. (1991). Mapping the margins: Intersectionality, identity politics, and
violence against women of color. *Stanford Law Review*, *43*, 1241–1299. https://
doi.org/10.2307/1229039 *Criminal Code*, RSC 1985, c C-46.

Cusmano, D. (2018). Rape culture rooted in patriarchy, media portrayal, and victim blaming. *Writing Across the Curriculum*. 30. https://digitalcommons.sacredheart.edu/wac_prize/30

Davison, C. (2016, October 12). The law of sexual assault in Canada. *Law Now Magazine*. www.lawnow.org/the-law-of-sexual-assault-in-canada/

Deer, S. (2015). *The beginning and end of rape: Confronting sexual violence in native America*. University of Minnesota Press.

de Heer, B., & Jones, L. (2017). Measuring sexual violence on campus: Climate surveys and vulnerable groups. *Journal of School Violence*, *16*(2), 207–221. https://doi.org/10.1080/15388220.2017.1284444

Deming, M. E., Covan, E. K., Swan, S. C., & Billings, D. L. (2013). Exploring rape myths, gendered norms, group processing, and the social context of rape among college women: A qualitative analysis. *Violence against Women*, *19*(4), 465–465. https://doi.org/10.1177/1077801213487044

Doolittle, R. (2017, February 3). Unfounded: Why police dismiss 1 in 5 sexual assault claims as baseless. *The Globe and Mail*. www.theglobeandmail.com/news/investigations/unfounded-sexual-assault-canada-main/article33891309/

Doolittle, R., Pereira, M., Agius, J., & Blenkinsop, L. (2017, December 8). Unfounded: What is your police service doing about sexual assault? *The Globe and Mail*. www.theglobeandmail.com/news/investigations/unfounded-what-is-your-police-service-doing-about-sexual-assault/article37245075/

Dylan, A., Regehr, C., & Alaggia, R. (2008). And justice for all? Aboriginal victims of sexual violence. *Violence against Women*, *14*(6), 678–696. https://doi.org/10.1177/1077801208317291

Edwards, K., Turchik, J., Dardis, C., Reynolds, N., & Gidycz, C. (2011). Rape myths: History, individual and institutional-level presence, and implications for change. *Sex Roles*, *65*(11–12), 761–773. https://doi.org/10.1007/s11199-011-9943-2

Elliott, D. M., Mok, D. S., & Briere, J. (2004). Adult sexual assault: Prevalence, symptomatology, and sex differences in the general population. *Journal of Traumatic Stress*, *17*(3), 203–211. https://doi.org/10.1023/B:JOTS.0000029263.11104.23

EVABC. (2016, May). Sexual assault support worker handbook. *Ending Violence BC*. https://endingviolence.org/publications/sexual-assault-support-worker-handbook/

Filipovic, J. (2008). Offensive feminism: The conservative gender norms that perpetuate rape culture, and how feminists can fight back. In *Yes means yes! Visions of female sexual power & a world without rape* (pp. 13–27). Seal Press. http://theconsentworkshop.com/wpcontent/uploads/2019/02/Jaclyn-Friedman-Jessica-Valenti-Yes-Means-Yes_-Visions-of-Female-Sexual-Power-and-A-World-Without-Rape-2008-Seal-Press.pdf

Fisher, B. S., Daigle, L. E., & Cullen, F. T. (2010). Creating safe havens: Preventing sexual victimization. In *Unsafe in the ivory tower: The sexual victimization of college women*. Sage Publications, Inc.

Flack, W. F., Caron, M. L., Leinen, S. J., Breitenbach, K. G., Barber, A. M., Brown, E. N., Gilbert, C. T., Harchak, T. F., Hendricks, M. M., Rector, C. E., Schatten, H. T., & Stein, H. C. (2008). "The red zone": Temporal risk for unwanted sex among college students. *Journal of Interpersonal Violence*, *23*(9),

1177–1177. *Journal of Interpersonal Violence*, *23*(9), 1177–1196. https://doi.org/10.1177/0886260508314308

Gannon, M., & Mihorean, K. (2005, November 24). Criminal victimisation in Canada, 2004. *Juristat 25*(7) (Statistics Canada Catalogue no. 85–002-XPE). https://www150.statcan.gc.ca/n1/pub/85-002-x/85-002-x2005007-eng.pdf

Garcia, C., & Vemuri, A. (2017). Theorizing "rape culture": How law, policy, and education can support and end sexual violence. *Education & Law Journal*, *27*(1), 1–17. www.proquest.com/scholarly-journals/theorizing-rape-culture-how-law-policy-education/docview/1983614241/se-2

Gartner, R., & Doob, A. N. (1994, June). Trends in criminal victimisation: 1988–1993. *Juristat 14*(13) (Statistics Canada Catalogue no. 85–002). www.ojp.gov/ncjrs/virtual-library/abstracts/trends-criminal-victimization-1988-1993

Government of Canada. (2021, June 4). *The Criminal Code of Canada*. Government of Canada, Department of Justice, Electronic Communications. https://www.justice.gc.ca/eng/csj-sjc/ccc/index.html#:~:text=The%20Criminal%20Code%20is%20a,improve%20the%20Canadian%20criminal%20process

Grady, C. (2017, November 30). The complicated, inadequate language of sexual violence. *Vox*. www.vox.com/culture/2017/11/30/16644394/language-sexual-violence

Greenland, J., & Cotter, A. (2018, July 23). Unfounded criminal incidents in Canada, 2017. *Juristat* (Statistics Canada Catalogue no. 85–002-X). https://www150.statcan.gc.ca/n1/pub/85-002-x/2018001/article/54975-eng.pdf

Griner, S. B., Vamos, C. A., Thompson, E. L., Logan, R., Vázquez-Otero, C., & Daley, E. M. (2017). The intersection of gender identity and violence: Victimisation experienced by transgender college students. *Journal of Interpersonal Violence*, *35*(23–24), 5704–5725. https://journals.sagepub.com/doi/pdf/10.1177/0886260517723743

Grubb, A., & Turner, E. (2012). Attribution of blame in rape cases: A review of the impact of rape myth acceptance, gender role conformity and substance use on victim blaming. *Aggression and Violent Behavior*, *17*(5), 443–452. https://doi.org/10.1016/j.avb.2012.06.002

Harber, K. D., Podolski, P., & Williams, C. H. (2015). Emotional disclosure and victim-blaming. *Emotion*, *15*(5), 1–12. www.researchgate.net/publication/274010621_Emotional_Disclosure_and_Victim_Blaming

Harris, C. J., & Linder, C. (2017). *Introduction. In Intersections of identity and sexual violence on campus: Centering minoritized students' experiences*. Stylus Publishing, LLC.

Heidinger, L. (2022, April 26). Violent victimisation and perceptions of safety: Experiences of first nations, métis and inuit women in Canada. *Juristat* (Statistics Canada Catalogue no. 85–002-X). https://www150.statcan.gc.ca/n1/pub/85-002-x/2022001/article/00004-eng.htm

Hildebrand, M. M., & Najdowski, C. J. (2015). The potential impact of rape culture on juror decision making: Implications for wrongful acquittals in sexual assault trials. *Albany Law Review*, *78*(3). https://web.s.ebscohost.com/ehost/pdfviewer/pdfviewer?vid=1&sid=de392fe0-8f1a-4e0d-8dae-4c538f4cc55e%40redis

Hill Collins, P., & Bilge, S. (2016). *Intersectionality*. Polity Press.

Holland, K. J., & Cortina, L. M. (2017). "It happens to girls all the time": Examining sexual assault survivors' reasons for not using campus supports. *American Journal of Community Psychology, 59*(1–2), 50–64. https://onlinelibrary.wiley.com/doi/abs/10.1002/ajcp.12126

Hong, L., & Marine, S. B. (2018). Sexual violence through a social justice paradigm: Framing and applications. *New Directions for Student Services, 2018*(161), 21–33. https://doi.org/10.1002/ss.20250

Hotton Mahony, T., Jacob, J., & Hobson, H. (2017). *Women in the criminal justice system.* Women in Canada: A Gender-based Statistical Report (Statistics Canada Catalogue no. 89–503-X). https://www150.statcan.gc.ca/n1/pub/89-503-x/89-503-x2015001-eng.htm

Humphreys, C. J., & Towl, G. J. (2020). *Addressing student sexual violence in higher education: A good practice guide.* Emerald Publishing Limited.

Hutchins, H. (2013). Risk factors for violence against women. In M. Sinha (Ed.), *Measuring violence against women: Statistical trends. Juristat (33)*1. (Statistics Canada Catalogue no. 85–002-X). https://www150.statcan.gc.ca/n1/pub/85-002-x/2013001/article/11766/11766-2-eng.htm

Ibrahim, D. (2018, April 12). Violent victimisation, discrimination and perceptions of safety: An immigrant perspective, Canada, 2014. *Juristat* (Statistics Canada Catalogue no. 85–002-X). https://www150.statcan.gc.ca/n1/pub/85-002-x/2018001/article/54911-eng.htm

Jaffray, B. (2020, September 9). Experiences of violent victimisation and unwanted sexual behaviours among gay, lesbian, bisexual and other sexual minority people, and the transgender population, in Canada, 2018. *Juristat* (Statistics Canada Catalogue no. 85–002-X). https://www150.statcan.gc.ca/n1/en/pub/85-002-x/2020001/article/00009-eng.pdf?st=I2gcP3DM

James, S. E., Herman, J. L., Rankin, S., Keisling, M., Mottet, L., & Anafi, M. (2016). *The report of the 2015 U.S. transgender survey.* National Center for Transgender Equality. https://transequality.org/sites/default/files/docs/usts/USTS-Full-Report-Dec17.pdf

Johnson, B. E., Kuck, D. L., & Schander, P. R. (1997). Rape myth acceptance and sociodemographic characteristics: A multidimensional analysis. *Sex Roles: A Journal of Research, 36*(11–12), 693–707. https://doi.org/10.1023/A:1025671021697

Johnson, H. (2012). Limits of a criminal justice response: Trends in police and court processing of sexual assault. In E. A. Sheehy (Ed.), *Sexual assault in Canada: Law, legal practice and women's activism* (pp. 613–634). University of Ottawa Press. https://books.openedition.orgupp/592

Johnson, H., Colpitts, E., Large, M., Parent, C., Denis, A., Baker, S., Singh, L., Christiansen-Ruffman, L., Edge, L., Kouldri, S., Lippman, A., Porter, M., & Stienstra, D. (2013, September 17). *Fact sheet: Violence against women in Canada.* Canadian Research Institute for the Advancement of Women (CRIAW). www.criaw-icref.ca/images/userfiles/files/VAW_ENG_longFinal.pdf

Karjane, M. H., Fisher, S. B., & Cullen, T. F. (2002). *Campus sexual assault: How America's institutions of higher education respond.* Final Report, NIJ Grant #1999-WA-VX-0008. Education Development Center, Inc. https://www.ncjrs.gov/pdffiles1/nij/grants/196676.pdf

Kaufman, M. (2008). Care of the adolescent sexual assault victim. *Pediatrics*, *122*(2), 462–470. https://doi.org/10.1542/peds.2008-1581

Khan, F., & Sweet, A. (2020). *Summaries: Statistics Canada's Recent reports on Gender-Based Violence and Public Safety*. https://www.couragetoact.ca/blog/statscansummaries

Khosla, P., & Barth, B. (2008). *Gender in local government: A sourcebook for trainers*. United Nations Human Settlements Programme. www.un.org/womenwatch/directory/pdf/Source_BK_9-May.pdf

Kimble, M., Neacsiu, A. D., Flack, W. F., & Horner, J. (2008). Risk of unwanted sex for college women: Evidence for a red zone. *Journal of American College Health*, *57*(3), 331–338. https://doi.org/10.3200/JACH.57.3.331-338

Kong, R., Johnson, H., Beattie, S., & Cardillo, A. (2003, July). Sexual offences in Canada. *Juristat 23*(6) (Statistics Canada Catalogue no. 85–002-XIE). https://www150.statcan.gc.ca/n1/pub/85-002-x/85-002-x2003006-eng.pdf

Krebs, C. P., Lindquist, C. H., Warner, T. D., Fisher, B. S., & Martin, S. L. (2007). *The campus sexual assault (CSA) study*. National Institute of Justice. www.ncjrs.gov/pdffiles1/nij/grants/221153.pdf

Lakin Afolabi Law. (2022, April 14). *What is the difference between sexual assault and rape?* https://lakinafolabilaw.com/difference-between-sexual-assault-and-rape-lakin-afolabi-law/

Lee, M. (2020, February 28). Nipissing task force tackles sexual violence survey results. *North Bay Nugget*. www.nugget.ca/news/local-news/nipissing-task-force-tackles-sexual-violence-survey-results

Lisak, D., Gardinier, L., Nicksa, S. C., & Cote, A. M. (2010). False allegations of sexual assault: An analysis of ten years of reported cases. *Violence against Women*, *16*(12), 1318–1334. https://doi.org/10.1177/1077801210387747

Lisak, D., & Miller, P. (2002). Repeat rape and multiple offending among undetected rapists. *Violence and Victims*, *17*(1), 73–84. https://time.com/wp-content/uploads/2014/09/repeat_rape.pdf

Lonsway, K. A., Banyard, V. L., Berkowitz, A. D., Gidycz, C. A., & Katz, J. T. (2009). *Rape prevention and risk reduction: Review of the research literature for practitioners*. The National Online Resource Center on Violence against Women. https://vawnet.org/sites/default/files/materials/files/2016-09/AR_RapePrevention.pdf

Lonsway, K. A., & Fitzgerald, L. F. (1994). Rape myths: In review. *Psychology of Women Quarterly*, *18*(2), 133–164. https://doi.org/10.1111/j.1471-6402.1994.tb00448.x

Luce, H., Schrager, S., & Gilchrist, V. (2010). Sexual assault of women. *American Family Physician*, *81*(4), 489–495. PMID: 20148503. https://pubmed.ncbi.nlm.nih.gov/20148503/

MacKinnon, C., & Hayden, P. (2001). Rape, genocide, and women's human rights. In *The philosophy of human rights*. Paragon House.

Martell Consulting Services Ltd. (2014). *Student safety in Nova Scotia: A review of student union policies and practices to prevent sexual violence*. www.studentsns.ca/s/2014-05-09-sexual-assault-report-KB-for-web1.pdf

Marx, B. P., Forsyth, J. P., Gallup, G. G., Fusé, T., & Lexington, J. M. (2008). Tonic immobility as an evolved predator defense: Implications for sexual assault survivors. *Clinical Psychology: Science and Practice*, *15*(1), 74–90. https://doi. org/10.1111/j.1468-2850.2008.00112.x

McGill University. (2015, April 24). *Sexual assault misconceptions*. McGill University Office for Sexual Violence Response, Support and Education. www.mcgill. ca/osvrse/survivor-support-self-care/misconceptions-vs-facts/misconceptions

McMahon, S., & Farmer, G. L. (2011). An updated measure for assessing subtle rape myths. *Social Work Research*, *35*(2), 71–81. www.jstor.org/stable/42659785

Meer, T., & Combrinck, H. (2015). Invisible intersections: Understanding the complex stigmatisation of women with intellectual disabilities in their vulnerability to gender-based violence. *Agenda*, *29*(2), 14–23. https://doi.org/10.1080/101309 50.2015.1039307

Merry, S. E. (2009). *Gender violence: A cultural perspective. Introductions to engaged anthropology*. Blackwell Publishing.

Metropolitan Action Committee on Violence Against Women. (2016, September 23). *Campus safety: Considerations and promising practices*. House of Commons Canada. www.ourcommons.ca/Content/Committee/421/FEWO/Brief/ BR8449919/br-external/METRAC-e.pdf

Mewett, A. W. (1993). The Canadian criminal code, 1892–1992. *Canadian Bar Review*, *72*(1), 1–27. https://cbr.cba.org/index.php/cbr/article/view/3634

Mitchell, K. J., Ybarra, M. L., & Korchmaros, J. D. (2014). Sexual harassment among adolescents of different sexual orientations and gender identities. *Child Abuse & Neglect*, *38*(2). https://reader.elsevier.com/reader/sd/pii/S01452134- 13002627?token=59AC06E46AE44512715B8F51BD0C2EEC0FC6C0269356B 1944C7A4139A3CD59809CC11F5027136D9151972A9BD11FD31A&originR egion=us-east-1&originCreation=20220911044616

Moreau, G. (2019, July 22). Police-reported crime statistics in Canada, 2018. *Juristat* (Statistics Canada Catalogue no. 85–002-X). https://www150.statcan.gc.ca/ n1/pub/85-002-x/2019001/article/00013-eng.htm

Moreau, G. (2022, August 3). Police-reported crime statistics in Canada, 2021. *Juristat* (Statistics Canada Catalogue no. 85–002-X). https://www150.statcan.gc.ca/ n1/pub/85-002-x/2022001/article/00013-eng.pdf

Morgan, R. E., & Truman, J. L. (2017). *Criminal victimization, 2017*. U.S Department of Justice NCJ 252472. https://bjs.ojp.gov/content/pub/pdf/cv17.pdf

Nelson, J. (2017). Storying gendered violence: Indigenous understandings of the interconnectedness of violence. *Social Justice and Community Engagement*, *24*. https://scholars.wlu.ca/cgi/viewcontent.cgi?article=1025&context=brantford_sjce

Nosek, M. A., Foley, C. C., Hughes, R. B., & Howland, C. A. (2001). Vulnerabilities for abuse among women with disabilities. *Sexuality and Disability: A Journal Devoted to the Psychological and Medical Aspects of Sexuality in Rehabilitation and Community Settings*, *19*(3), 177–189. https://doi.org/10.1023/A:1013152530758

Ontario Native Women's Association (ONWA). (2011). After healing is healthy living: Consultation on sexual violence and Aboriginal community. *Catalyst Research and Communications*, *26*. www.onwa.ca/upload/documents/consulta- tion-on-sexual-violence-report.pdf

Payne, D. L., Lonsway, K. A., & Fitzgerald, L. F. (1999). Rape myth acceptance: Exploration of its structure and its measurement using the Illinois rape myth acceptance scale. *Journal of Research in Personality*, *33*(1), 27–68. https://doi.org/10.1006/jrpe.1998.2238

Perez, Z. J., & Hussey, H. (2014). A hidden crisis: Including the LGBT community when addressing sexual violence on college campuses. *Center for American Progress*. www.americanprogress.org/article/a-hidden-crisis/

Perreault, S. (2015, November 23). Criminal victimisation in Canada, 2014. *Juristat* (Statistics Canada Catalogue no. 85–002-X). https://www150.statcan.gc.ca/n1/pub/85-002-x/2015001/article/14241-eng.pdf

Perreault, S. (2022, July 19). Victimisation of first nations people, Métis and Inuit in Canada. *Juristat* (Statistics Canada Catalogue no. 85–002-X). https://www150.statcan.gc.ca/n1/pub/85-002-x/2022001/article/00012-eng.htm

Perreault, S., & Brennan, S. (2010, September 28). Criminal victimisation in Canada, 2009. *Juristat 30*(2) (Statistics Canada Catalogue no. 85–002-X). https://www150.statcan.gc.ca/n1/pub/85-002-x/2010002/article/11340-eng.pdf

Primeau, C. (n.d.). *Celebrating women: Bill C-127*. https://atrium.lib.uoguelph.ca/xmlui/bitstream/handle/10214/17837/Primeau_Jayasankar_BillC127_RSP3_2020.pdf?sequence=4&isAllowed=y#:~:text=In%201983%2C%20Bill%20C%2D127,the%20offences%20of%20sexual%20assault

Quinlan, E. (2017). Introduction: Sexual violence in the ivory tower. In E. Quinlan, A. Quinlan, C. Fogel, & G. Taylor (Eds.), *Sexual violence at Canadian universities: Activism, institutional responses, and strategies for change* (pp. 1–24). ProQuest Ebook Central. https://ebookcentral.proquest.com

Ridgeway, S. (2014, March 10). 25 everyday examples of rape culture. *Everyday Feminism*. http://everydayfeminism.com/2014/03/examples-of-rape-culture/

Rotenberg, C. (2017a, October 3). Police-reported sexual assaults in Canada, 2009 to 2014: A statistical profile. *Juristat* (Statistics Canada Catalogue no. 85–002-X). https://www150.statcan.gc.ca/n1/pub/85-002-x/2017001/article/54866-eng.pdf

Rotenberg, C. (2017b, October 26). From arrest to conviction: Court outcomes of police-reported sexual assaults in Canada, 2009 to 2014. *Juristat* (Statistics Canada Catalogue no. 85–002-X). https://www150.statcan.gc.ca/n1/pub/85-002-x/2017001/article/54870-eng.htm

Rotenberg, C. (2019, July 4). Police-reported violent crimes against young women and girls in Canada's Provincial North and Territories, 2017. *Juristat* (Statistics Canada Catalogue no. 85–002-X). https://www150.statcan.gc.ca/n1/pub/85-002-x/2019001/article/00012-eng.htm

Rotenberg, C., & Cotter, A. (2018, November 8). Police-reported sexual assaults in Canada before and after #MeToo, 2016 and 2017. *Juristat* (Statistics Canada Catalogue no. 85–002-X). https://www150.statcan.gc.ca/n1/pub/85-002-x/2018001/article/54979-eng.htm

Rothman, E. F., Exner, D., & Baughman, A. L. (2011). The prevalence of sexual assault against people who identify as gay, lesbian, or bisexual in the United States: A systematic review. *Trauma, Violence & Abuse*, *12*(2), 55–66. https://doi.org/10.1177/1524838010390707

R. v. Chase, [1987] 2 S.C.R. 293.

R. v. Ewanchuk [1999] 1 S.C.R. 330.

Sable, M. R., Danis, F., Mauzy, D. L., & Gallagher, S. K. (2006). Barriers to reporting sexual assault for women and men: Perspectives of college students. *Journal of American College Health, 55*(3), 157–162. https://doi.org/10.3200/ JACH.55.3.157-162

Samples, T. (2015, May 7). *Rape culture is real.* Sojourners. https://sojo.net/articles/ rape-culture-real

Scott, M. (2017). Jake and Josie get drunk and hook up: An exploration of mutual intoxication and sexual assault. *Alberta Law Review, 54*(4). https:// albertalawreview.com/index.php/ALR/article/view/786/778

Senn, C. Y., Eliasziw, M., Barata, P. C., Thurston, W. E., Newby-Clark, I. R., Radtke, L., Hobden, K. L., & SARE Study Team. (2014). Sexual violence in the lives of first-year university women in Canada: No improvements in the 21st century. *BMC Women's Health, 14*, 135–143. https://doi.org/10.1186/ s12905-014-0135-4

Sexual Violence Prevention Committee (SVPC). (2017, December 15). *Changing the culture of acceptance: Recommendations to address sexual violence on university campuses.* Council of Nova Scotia University Presidents. https://novascotia.ca/lae/pubs/docs/changing-the-culture-of-acceptance.pdf

Shaffer, M. (2012). *The impact of the charter on the law of sexual assault: Plus ça change, plus c'est la même chose.* The Supreme Court Law Review: Osgoode's Annual Constitutional Cases Conference 57. https://digitalcommons.osgoode. yorku.ca/sclr/vol57/iss1/15

Shankar, I., & Tavcer, D. S. (2021). "Good people with good intentions": Deconstructing a post-secondary institution's sexual violence policy construction. *Canadian Journal of Educational Administration and Policy, 195*(195), 2–16. https://doi.org/10.7202/1075669a

Sheehy, E. A. (2000). Rape shield laws: Canada. In N. H. Rafter (Ed.), *Encyclopaedia of women and crime* (pp. 226–227). Oryx Press. https://ssrn.com/ abstract=2327393

Simpson, L. (2018, May 31). Violent victimisation of lesbians, gays and bisexuals in Canada, 2014. *Juristat* (Statistics Canada Catalogue no. 85–002-X). https:// www150.statcan.gc.ca/n1/pub/85-002-x/2018001/article/54923-eng.htm

Sinha, M. (2013, February 25). Prevalence and severity of violence against women. In M. Sinha (Ed.), Measuring violence against women: Statistical trends. *Juristat 30*(1) (Statistics Canada Catalogue no. 85–002-X). https://www150.statcan.gc.ca/ n1/pub/85-002-x/2013001/article/11766-eng.pdf

Sinha, M. (2015, June 22). Trends in reporting criminal victimisation to police, 1999 to 2009. *Juristat* (Statistics Canada Catalogue no. 85–002-X). https://www150. statcan.gc.ca/n1/pub/85-002-x/2015001/article/14198-eng.pdf

Skrypnek, J. (2021, April 9). Explainer: What is rape culture and what does it look like in B.C.? *Langley Advance Times.* www.langleyadvancetimes.com/news/ explainer-what-is-rape-culture-and-what-does-it-look-like-on-b-c/

Spiwak, R., & Brownridge, D. A. (2005). Separated women's risk for violence: An analysis of the Canadian Situation. *Journal of Divorce & Remarriage, 43*(3/4), 105–117.

Somerville, M. A., & Gall, G. L. (2012, February 6). Sexual assault. *The Canadian Encyclopedia.* www.thecanadianencyclopedia.ca/en/article/sexual-assault

Statistics Canada. (2016). *Uniform crime reporting manual.* Surveys and Statistical Programs. Canadian Centre for Justice Statistics.

Statistics Canada. (2020, September 14). One in ten women students sexually assaulted in a post-secondary setting. *The Daily* (Statistics Canada Catalogue no. 11–001-X). https://www150.statcan.gc.ca/n1/daily-quotidien/200914/dq200914a-eng.htm

Statistics Canada. (2022, July 9). Criminal victimisation of First Nations, Métis and Inuit people in Canada, 2018 to 2020. *The Daily* (Statistics Canada). https://www150.statcan.gc.ca/n1/daily-quotidien/220719/dq220719c-eng.htm

Tang, K. (1998). Rape law reform in Canada: The success and limits of legislation. *International Journal of Offender Therapy and Comparative Criminology, 42*(3), 258–270. https://doi.org/10.1177/0306624X9804200307

Tjaden, P., & Thoenees, N. (2000). *Prevalence, incidence, and consequences of violence against women: Findings from the national violence against women survey.* U.S Department of Justice. https://www.ncjrs.gov/pdffiles1/nij/183781.pdf

Trainor, C., & Mihorean, K. (2001, June 28). Family violence in Canada: A statistical profile, 2001. *Ministry of Industry* (Statistics Canada Catalogue no. 85–224-XIE). https://www150.statcan.gc.ca/n1/en/pub/85-224-x/85-224-x2001000-eng.pdf?st=hiHiqRV4

United States Department of Justice. (2005). *Sexual assault on campus: What colleges and universities are doing about it.* U.S Department of Justice National Institute of Justice https://www.ncjrs.gov/pdffiles1/nij/205521.pdf

VanTassel, B. (2020, January). *Culture and perspectives on a sexual assault policy.* www.msvu.ca/wp-content/uploads/2020/11/2020-CAPSAP-Report-1.pdf

Venema, R. M. (2016). Police officer schema of sexual assault reports: Real rape, ambiguous cases, and false reports. *Journal of Interpersonal Violence, 31*(5), 872–899. https://doi.org/10.1177/0886260514556765

Weikle, B. (2016, September 13). Universities face increasing pressure to address campus sexual assault. *CBC News.* www.cbc.ca/news/canada/campus-sexual-assault-1.3750355

Women and Gender Equality Canada. (2018). *About gender-based violence.* https://femmes-egalite-genres.canada.ca/en/gender-based-violence-knowledge-centre/about-gender-based-violence.html

World Health Organization & Pan American Health Organization. (2012). *Understanding and addressing violence against women: Sexual violence.* www.paho.org/hq/dmdocuments/2012/paho-violence-women-fs-sv-2012.pdf

3 Understanding consent education

Vicky Dobkins and D. Scharie Tavcer

Introduction

For decades, Canadian post-secondary institutions (PSIs) have been trying to address the prevalence of sexual violence (SV) through policies and processes. Still, students remain disproportionately at risk (Canadian Federation of Students - Ontario, 2015). SV affects as many as 33% of Canadian female university students (DeKeseredy et al., 1993; Newton-Taylor et al., 1998; Quinlan, 2017), and Conroy & Cotter (2017) identified that secondary and post-secondary students reported 41% of all sexual assaults. A key characteristic of SV is the absence of consent (Beres, 2007; Jaffe et al., 2021; Moyano et al., 2022). However, sexual consent is an intricate concept, and its definitions vary greatly among legal, academic, and popular domains (Benoit & Ronis, 2022; Dixie, 2017).

Because sexual consent is highly contextual, many factors can convolute students' understanding. Legislation, media, rape culture, stereotypes, peers, sociocultural aspects, and inaccurate information all influence how sexual consent is understood, accepted, and practised. A paradigm shift prompted by women's organisations in the 1990s pressured lawmakers and PSIs to address the misunderstandings of consent (Shaffer, 2012). With universities already receiving immense criticism for not doing enough to prevent SV on campuses (Krause et al., 2017; MacDougall et al., 2020), efforts to implement interventions and education were subsequently reactive, impetuous, focused on singular (not comprehensive) approaches (Hovick & Silver, 2019; Katz & Moore, 2013; Thiessen et al., 2021; Thomas et al., 2016).

The incorporation of sexual consent education into policies and programming in PSIs can be a powerful tool in the reduction of SV, but past and current prevention efforts have shown inconsistent results and are currently not regulated, evaluated, or mandated for most provinces in Canada (Heenehan, 2019; Katz & Moore, 2013; Thiessen et al., 2021; Thomas et al., 2016).

DOI: 10.4324/9781003332671-3

This chapter aims to provoke our understanding of sexual consent and its relevance to sexual consent education. It identifies three significant components: sexual violence, sexual consent, and sexual consent education and it evaluates how these concepts interconnect and inform each other.

Rape culture

A major contributing factor to the convolution of students' understanding of sexual consent is rape culture. Rape culture is a form of structural violence found in almost any arena of society (i.e., media, social media, education, politics, justice, and more). It invokes the normalisation of misogyny and

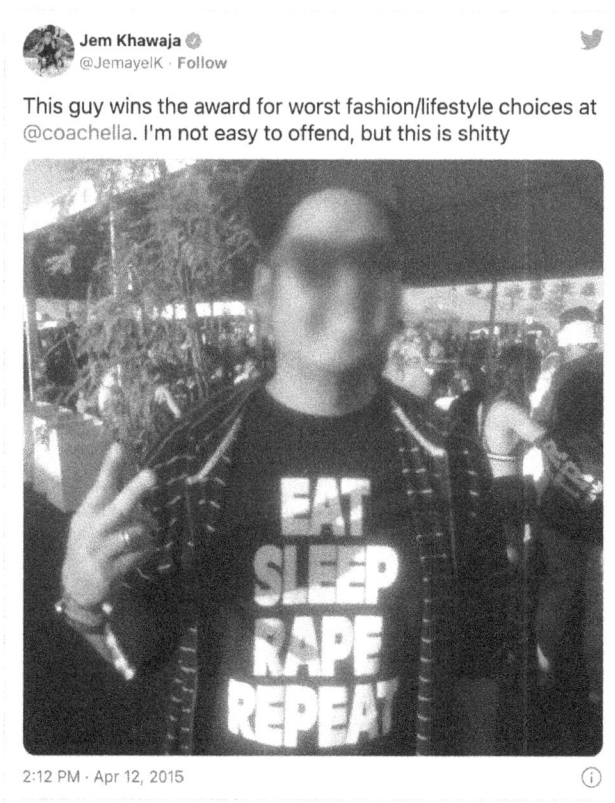

Figure 3.1 A young man proudly wears a pro-rape T-shirt at the Coachella music festival in 2015.

Source: @JemayelK [Twitter] with permission.

SV (Bourassa et al., 2017; Skrypnek, 2021; VanTassel, 2020) and enforces the belief that rape is inevitable and it is the responsibility of the individual (i.e., women) to prevent its occurrence (Cusmano, 2018; Edwards et al., 2011; Filipovic, 2008; MacKinnon, 2001; SVPC, 2017). Although the constructs of rape culture were discussed in Chapter 2, it is reiterated here as it presents a slightly different way within a post-secondary context. Most students are not oblivious to the alarmingly high prevalence rate of SV on campuses. Still, due to the omnipresence of rape culture and the pressure to party and consume drugs and alcohol, students appear desensitised and go along with the idea that campus sexual assault (CSA) is unavoidable and even acceptable (MacDougall et al., 2020; Salvino et al., 2017).

Orientation weeks at PSIs are often championed as a glorified opportunity for students to experiment and push their boundaries, creating situations fraught with risks. Alcohol and drug consumption also increases the risk of SV as some will use it to incapacitate potential victims; some use it to justify their actions; and some will use it to shame and blame victims (Haskell, 2011; Jacobs, 2021; Martell Consulting Services Ltd., 2014; Scott & Graves, 2017; Quinlan, 2017). Orientation weeks are a perilous time for students; also known as the *red zone*, a term which refers to the first eight weeks of the school year when there is heightened alcohol and drug consumption, parties, and an uptick in SV (The Fulcrum, 2018; McCabe, 2018). Studies show that of all the sexual assaults that take place on post-secondary campuses during the academic year, more than 50% will take place during the first two months of classes (Bourassa et al., 2017; Canadian Federation of Students Ontario, 2015; Martell Consulting Services Ltd., 2014; Salvino et al., 2017). Despite decades of research linking orientation week parties to increased incidents of gender based violence (GBV), they are not deterred or curtailed (Orchard, 2021).

This is particularly evident in PSIs, with fraternities and sororities embedded with hundreds of years of culture that facilitates and perpetuates sexism and violence. For example, sororities (for women) are not permitted to host parties with alcohol despite the students being of legal drinking age. At the same time, fraternities (for men) are allowed to host with alcohol. Since sororities cannot throw such parties, they collaborate with fraternities, making the two organisations co-dependent. This means that off-campus parties are almost exclusively thrown by male-only organisations controlled by fraternity brothers who monitor the door, dictate which attendees are worthy of entering, and control the types and amounts of alcohol served (Jackson, 2018; Marzell et al., 2015; Shupe, 2022). The combination of toxic masculine environments with excessive partying and heavy alcohol and drug consumption facilitates SV (Armstrong et al., 2006; SVPC, 2017); research shows that sorority women and fraternity men are more likely than other students to be survivors and perpetrators, respectively, of sexual assault (Bannon et al., 2013; Boswell & Spade, 1996; Dixie, 2017; Lanza-Kaduce et al., 2006).

Fraternities foster rape culture and rape myths, which in turn dissolves consent. One example is a chant from pledges (men competing to join a fraternity) in the Yale chapter of Delta Kappa Epsilon. In the fall of 2010, pledges were marched blindfolded past a dormitory that housed women. While marching, they chanted, "No means yes, and yes means anal!" and other X-rated poetry expressing a desire to have sex with dead women (Allen, 2011).

Rape culture on campuses can be overtly expressed (with blatant pro-rape chants) or subtly expressed (through victim blaming). One pro-rape chant took place on a bus ride during a three-day orientation party hosted by the Sauder School of Business at the University of British Columbia in 2013. "Y-O-U-N-G at UBC! We like 'em young! Y is for your sister, O is for oh so tight, U is for underage, N is for no consent, G is for go to jail" (CBC News, 2013). Nuances of rape culture on campuses are exemplified through rape myths. The danger of rape myths within the context of PSIs is that those who subscribe to them may very well not know, such as the nature and power of a myth (Humphreys & Towl, 2020). Rape myths are societal misconceptions about sexual assault used to minimise or justify rape, blame victims, and absolve perpetrators of guilt (Humphreys & Towl, 2020). Victim blaming employs the idea that victims are responsible for their safety and the unwanted, negative attention they receive (Dixie, 2017).

Another rape myth is the belief that sexual assaults are often perpetrated by strangers (Linder, 2018). Within the context of PSIs, this rape myth constructs perpetrators of SV as non-students ("strangers") and illustrates how rape culture and SV can be institutionally embedded (Ahmed, 2017; Colpitts, 2019; Gray & Pin, 2017; Linder, 2018). PSIs capitalise upon false assumptions about stranger sexual assault to protect and enhance their brand (Grey & Pin, 2017), when in fact, a 2019 Statistics Canada study exploring students' experiences of SV in Canadian PSIs revealed that most women (80%) and men (86%) who had experienced unwanted sexualised behaviours stated that the perpetrators of the behaviours were fellow students (Burczycka, 2020).

Rape myths create barriers to establishing sexual consent (Johnson & Hoover, 2015); as evidenced by one of the most endorsed rape myths (20%), *he didn't mean to [commit rape]* (Vandiver & Dupalo, 2013). This presupposes the belief that SV happens only when people misunderstand each other (Deming et al., 2013; Harris, 2018; Johnson & Hoover, 2015; Vandiver & Dupalo, 2013), but scholars have undermined the validity of this hypothesis (Adams-Curtis & Forbes, 2004; Harris, 2018; Kitzinger & Frith, 1999).

Figure 3.2 Campaign poster to challenge rape culture by Draw-the-Line.
Source: http://draw-the-line.ca/resources/wr-frosh.html

When an individual does not understand that consent is mandatory and their belief in rape myths is pervasive, these conflate and result in a mistaken belief of consent and a misguided justification or rationalisation for SV.

Susceptibility to the acceptance of rape myths and rape culture is influenced by one's social, economic, cultural, and racial positionality, which directly correlates to whether an individual engages in consent behaviours (Richmond & Peterson, 2020; Shumlich & Fisher, 2019). Structural and cultural changes are needed to dismantle rape culture, particularly regarding understanding sexual consent.

Definition of consent in Canadian law

In 1992, Bill C-49, *An Act to amend the Criminal Code (sexual assault)*, was passed, resulting in changes that provided greater clarity and legal protection for complainants. Bill C-49 introduced Section 273.1 in the *Criminal Code*, which amended the statute in three significant ways (Government of Canada, 2021; Shaffer, 2012):

(1) It provided a definition of consent.
(2) It included a non-exhaustive list of situations in which consent cannot be obtained, and
(3) It added the defence of mistaken belief in consent.

Section 273.1(1) defines consent as the voluntary agreement of individuals to engage in the sexual activity in question. Conduct short of a voluntary agreement to engage in sexual activity does not constitute consent. A voluntary agreement is stipulated in that *no* consent is obtained as follows:

• Where the agreement is expressed by the words or conduct of a person other than the complainant.
• Where the complainant is incapable of consenting to the activity (e.g., because they are unconscious or asleep).
• Where the perpetrator induces the complainant to engage in the activity by abusing a position of trust, power, or authority.
• Where the complainant expresses, by words or conduct, a lack of agreement to engage in the activity.
• Where the complainant, having consented to engage in sexual activity, expresses, by words or conduct, a lack of agreement to continue to engage in the activity.

Section 265(3) in the *Criminal Code* also clarifies the absence of consent. It states that no consent is obtained where the complainant submits or does not resist because of force or threats to them or a third person. Consent is absent when there are threats of bodily harm to the person or another, and consent is absent if it was obtained by fraud.

In Section 265(4), the statute instructs a judge to determine whether the defendant's claims are an honest belief or they had consent to engage in the behaviour in question. The defence of a mistaken belief in consent prompts whether the person seeking consent reasonably believed or had an honest belief they obtained consent. A person cannot claim this defence whether those beliefs arose from recklessness, wilful blindness, or where they failed to take reasonable steps to ascertain that there was consent. To dissect these elements is an exercise in criminal law and beyond the scope of this text, but for further exploration of this defence, see (CICS, 2018; Government of Canada, 2021; LEAF, 2020; Scott & Graves, 2017; Shaffer, 2012).

The case law that guides the decision making comes from *R. v. Ewanchuk* [1999] 1 S.C.R. 330, "the absence of consent, however, is subjective and determined by reference to the complainant's subjective internal state of mind towards the touching, at the time it occurred" (para. 26). The statute includes the word *voluntary* to reinforce the fact that sometimes victims say "yes" to the sexual activity in question because they are afraid, threatened, or coerced. Saying yes, under those circumstances, vitiates consent. Under Section 265(3), the question of whether consent has been obtained is determined through the subjective perspective of the victim and focuses on what the person was thinking and feeling at the time of the sexual assault (Lakin Afolabi Law, 2022; LEAF, 2020). The law also acknowledges the reality of sexual assault in that some people may freeze in response to what is happening, or they don't say "no," or they don't fight back, they flop, or even befriend their attacker. These responses are dictated by the person's limbic system in the brain responses (Center for Substance Abuse Treatment, 2014) and are normative responses to a traumatic experience. Victims will do whatever they must to survive the traumatic experience (Patterson & Campbell, 2010; Weiss, 2010).

General misconceptions continue to ensure that the law of sexual consent is sometimes ignored, sometimes misinterpreted, and often fails to achieve its promise (Vandervort, 2012). But realistically, few people know the law and how they learn about consent is through their peers, parents, or social and mainstream media (MacDougall et al., 2020). These sources, however, are filled with myths and stereotypes that convolute the language of consent and educate people inaccurately.

The language used in Sections 265(3) and 273.1 is concise and specific and reflects a new robust ideal of consent referred to as *affirmative consent*. Affirmative consent focuses on enthusiastic, precise, verbal communication (Muehlenhard et al., 2016). It relies on the presence of a *yes* when establishing sexual consent rather than a presence of a *no* (Johnson & Hoover, 2015). Silence or passivity does not equal consent (Muehlenhard et al., 2016). Affirmative consent is an active and ongoing process that includes accepting that consent can be revoked at any time, even in the middle of a sexual act. The onus to ascertain consent is placed on the person initiating the sexual encounter rather than the other party's responsibility to convey their non-consent (Shumlich & Fisher, 2019). Affirmative sexual consent is not an "emerging" standard; it has been recognised as an essential element of the common law and statutory definitions of sexual consent by the Supreme Court of Canada since 1994 (Vandervort, 2012). Bussel (2008) stated it best when she said, "we do everyone a service when we recognise that consent is not simply a legal term and should encompass more than simply yes or no" (p. 44).

Research and interventions are needed to address barriers that hinder young adults from establishing affirmative sexual consent (Johnson & Hoover, 2015). It is necessary to craft sexual consent practices that are not antagonistic to current sexual consent norms and coach behavioural skills development for implementing affirmative consent practices effectively (Shumlich & Fisher, 2019).

The language of consent

The language of consent and sexual communication is shaped by social and cultural factors (Benoit & Ronis, 2022; Brady et al., 2018; Johnson & Hoover, 2015), and with the definition of sexual consent being open to interpretation, there is much room for errors in communication between sexual partners (Dixie, 2017). An important factor in understanding the language of consent and sexual communication is the role of traditional sexual scripts. In 1973, Gagnon and Simon developed the Sexual Script Theory (SST) (Dixie, 2017; Gagnon & Simon, 1973). SST explains how individuals develop their understanding of expected sexual behaviours and how this influences real-life occurrences (Byers, 1996; Dixie, 2017; Jozkowski & Peterson, 2013; Krahé et al., 2000; Rose & Frieze, 1989, 1993).

Assumptions about gender roles are embedded in sexual scripts that prescribe men as unrelenting initiators of sexual encounters and women as the sexually reluctant gatekeepers (Byers, 1996; Cahill, 2017; Gagnon & Simon, 1973; Hust et al., 2017; Jozkowski et al., 2014; Krahé et al., 2000; MacDougall et al., 2020; Scott & Graves, 2017; Thiessen et al., 2021). Sexual scripts must be discussed in a gendered framework (Fenner, 2017), as gender roles influence the way sexual consent is understood by students (Brady et al., 2018). Sexual scripts are based on heteronormative narratives that enforce beliefs that women must satisfy men's sexual needs (Benoit &

Ronis, 2022; SVPC, 2017; Solomon, 2018) and widespread adherence to traditional and gendered sexual scripts not only informs personal behaviours but also informs expectations of one's sexual partner.

The language of consent and sexual communication is also shaped by rape culture and peer norms (Johnson & Hoover, 2015; Murnen et al., 2002). Research has shown that young adults feel pressured to adjust their behaviour and beliefs regarding sexual consent to align with the behaviour and beliefs of their peers (Dixie, 2017; Humphreys, 2004; Humphreys & Brousseau, 2010; Johnson & Hoover, 2015).

Insight into the roles of sexual scripts within sexual communication can help us to better understand the sociocultural aspects that contribute to high rates of sexual coercion and assault on campuses (Johnson & Hoover, 2015; MacDougall et al., 2020). Consent plays a crucial role in understanding SV, and there is much confusion and debate about what constitutes consensual sexual behaviour (Anderson, 2022; SVPC, 2017).

Understanding consent

The #MeToo movement was first established in 2006 by American activist Tarana Burke after her own experience of SV. The hashtag made international headlines in 2017. The #MeToo movement sparked powerful conversations about SV and the importance of consent, prompting women worldwide to share their stories (Garcia, 2017; MacDougall et al., 2020). In Canada, the #MeToo movement uncovered how much change was needed for everyone to understand consent and impelled service providers, employers, law enforcement, and educators to re-evaluate policies and procedures. This increased emphasis on sexual consent coincided with greater public awareness and support for survivors of SV (Beres, 2020; Mendes et al., 2018).

A study by Rotenberg and Cotter (2018) found there were more police-reported sexual assaults in 2017 than in any year since 1998; many police services in Canada cited #MeToo as a contributing factor to the increase in reported sexual assaults in their jurisdictions (Coubrough, 2018; Laframboise, 2017; Mehta, 2018; Smith, 2018; Winiewski, 2017). The age and gender profiles of victims were similar before (55%) and after (56%) #MeToo, with young women and girls under 25 years old continuing to have the highest rates of police-reported sexual assault (Rotenberg & Cotter, 2018). The upward trend of police reporting continues despite a slight dip occurring during the first year of the COVID-19 pandemic. In 2016, there were a total of 21,014 police-reported incidents of sexual assault, and in 2021, there were 34,242 (Keighley, 2017; Moreau, 2022). In the same period, the rates of self-reported sexual assaults (levels 1, 2, and 3) had also increased exponentially. Victimisation surveys pre and post #MeToo revealed 633,000 sexual assaults in 2014 and 940,000 in 2019 (Cotter, 2021; Perreault, 2015). Despite there being an increase in the number of reports to police, the research indicates that both 2018 and 2019 had the lowest percentage of sexual assaults reported to police since 1993 (5% and 6%, respectively) (Moreau, 2019; Moreau et al., 2020).

Although it seems like it would be safe to assume that the attention gained by #MeToo would have resulted in increased awareness and understanding of what sexual consent is and how its omission contributes to SV, it did just the opposite. Before the movement, a study by the Canadian Women's Foundation showed that only one in three Canadians knew what it meant to give sexual consent, and a follow-up survey conducted in 2018 revealed that Canadians' understanding of consent had, in fact, decreased (Canadian Women's Foundation, 2015, 2018). If the general population does not understand sexual consent, how can we expect this from students?

A failure to understand sexual consent has been linked to the perpetration of SV among undergraduate students (Thiessen et al., 2021), illustrating a need to evaluate how students define and practice sexual consent. Despite a multitude of research on SV, there is a deficit of literature on sexual consent (Dixie, 2017; Fenner, 2017) and how young adults obtain and provide sexual consent remains ambiguous (Benoit & Ronis, 2022; Beres, 2014; Muehlenhard et al., 2016). No consensus has been reached on what sexual consent is and how it should be communicated (Beres, 2007; Moyano et al., 2022; Righi et al., 2021). Muehlenhard et al. (2016) explain the complex nature of sexual consent:

> Consent can be conceptualized in numerous ways: as a feeling or decision, as an explicit agreement, or as behavior indicative of willingness; as something that can be assumed or as something that must be given explicitly; and as a discrete event or as an ongoing, continuous process. All this is further complicated by numerous factors: Individuals are often ambivalent or uncertain about what they want or are willing to do.
> (p. 482)

The 2018 Student Voices on Sexual Violence Survey (CCI Research Inc., 2019; Council of Ontario Universities, 2020) was conducted with 117,148 post-secondary students across Ontario, Canada. The survey consisted of five themes, including a Perceptions of Consent Index, which evaluated the opinions, attitudes, and beliefs about consent in various sexual situations (CCI Research Inc., 2019; Council of Ontario Universities, 2020). Student respondents were to indicate their level of agreement to statements such as "consent must be given at each step in a sexual encounter." Results showed that over 90% of participants stated they either agreed or strongly agreed, and it was concluded that respondents demonstrated a consistent and robust understanding of consent (Council of Ontario Universities, 2020).

In studies where students were asked to provide their definition of sexual consent, almost all participants could do so, but their context-free definitions varied significantly (Beres, 2014; 2020; Brady et al., 2018; Jozkowski et al., 2014; Muehlenhard et al., 2016; Ostridge & O'Connor, 2020; Thiessen et al., 2021). In the research project, this book centres around, most students were also able to define consent, but those definitions were not always fulsome or accurate (see Chapter 5). Students appear to default to descriptions of sexual consent as outlined in legal definitions and affirmative consent policies, but others focus their definitions solely on aspects of non-consent.

A study by Beres (2014) argued that understanding of consent was disconnected from how young people understood communication about sex. And when participants were using a language of consent, a "very different picture emerges – one where consent is but a minimum standard for acceptable or non-criminal sex" (p. 382). The literature reveals that students can identify specific characteristics of sexual consent but do not have a holistic understanding of the concept and its limitations in "real-life" settings (Beres, 2014; Fenner, 2017; Shumlich & Fisher, 2018).

Students also appear to have an overtly simplified perception of communication during sex (Beres, 2014) where clear, unambiguous, verbal communication about sexual consent is rarely used (Humphreys, 2004; Humphreys & Brousseau, 2010; Johnson & Hoover, 2015; Jozkowski et al., 2014; Shumlich & Fisher, 2018). Across studies, students reported they communicated consent by using nonverbal behaviours or by not resisting their partners' advances (Benoit & Ronis, 2022; Hall, 1998; Hickman & Muehlenhard, 1999; Jozkowski, 2013; Jozkowski et al., 2014; Jozkowski & Wiersma, 2015; Muehlenhard et al., 2016). In a study by Jozkowski et al. (2014), students identified a reliance on consent cues – including nonverbal cues, tone of voice, and text messaging (or "sexting") – but acknowledged, these could be difficult to decipher if they are ambiguous and vague. Most sexual encounters were stated to include indirect, veiled, and coded behaviours that require inference of sexual consent or non-consent (Shumlich & Fisher, 2018).

Students may feel reluctant to use explicit verbal consent communication cues because of social norms that people should not talk about sex or beliefs that explicit communication about sex is awkward (Curtis & Burnett, 2017; Willis et al., 2019). Consent communication may also deteriorate when students anticipate their partner's consent cues to be identical to their own (Hickman & Muehlenhard, 1999; Scott & Graves, 2017), but "when we passively respond or assume we know what the other person's thinking, we could very well be wrong" (Bussel, 2008), resulting in the perpetration of non-consensual sex (i.e., sexual assault) (Benoit & Ronis, 2022).

It should be noted that definitions of consent also vary depending on country and jurisdiction (Benoit & Ronis, 2022; Beres, 2014). Most of the available research on students' perceptions and understanding of sexual consent and sexual communication is based on populations in the USA and is contained within a heteronormative framework (Benoit & Ronis, 2022; Fenner, 2017; Rollo, n.d.). And studies conducted in Canada have noted that convenience samples of university undergraduates are not representative of the general population (Humphreys & Brousseau, 2010). Diverse educational and cultural backgrounds mean that university students have different notions of consent affected by factors such as their perception of consent cues, their conflation of willingness and acquiescence, and their perceptions of gender roles (Garcia & Vemuri, 2017).

Overall, many post-secondary students report only basic definitions of consent (Jozkowski et al., 2014; Thiessen et al., 2021), but this could also be attributed to poor quality sexual health education programming available to students prior to attending post-secondary schools. Due to the stigma surrounding sex and sexuality, the implementation of sexual health education has historically been met with much discourse. The values and norms surrounding sexuality can come from a variety of sources, including social and religious viewpoints, science, medicine, and individual experience (Public Health Agency of Canada, 2019), which can influence opinions of what schools can teach, what teachers are willing to teach, and what parents are willing to accept (Woodley et al., 2022).

Thiessen et al. (2021) explored what Canadian PSI students recall being taught about sexual consent before attending university. The study revealed that most students had expressed unmet needs regarding the sexual health education they received, describing a "lack of preparedness for engaging in healthy sexuality and relationships" (p. 354).

Currently, sexual health education programmes are failing many young Canadians and rendering them ill-prepared for when they enter post-secondary settings. Canadian universities may not be adequately filling the gap in sexual consent education left by secondary schools (Camp et al., 2018; MacDougall et al., 2020; Ortiz & Shafer, 2018), and in turn, sexual consent education in PSIs may be ill-equipped to address deficits in students' precollege sexual health education and sexual literacy (Hirsch et al., 2018).

Sexual consent education

Sexual consent education creates awareness of the statistical realities of the prevalence of SV on Canadian campuses. CSAs were first documented over 30 years ago, and the history of CSA prevention activism has been ongoing since the early 1980s (Forrest & Senn, 2017; Rollo, n.d.; Senn et al., 2017). Traditionally, SV prevention interventions in PSIs have been reactionary and have focused on singular (not comprehensive) approaches. These prevention efforts have shown inconsistent results in their abilities to change behaviour and fall short in addressing the causes and dynamics of SV (Heenehan, 2019; Katz & Moore, 2013; Thiessen et al., 2021; Thomas et al., 2016). Despite decades of increased campus security, social marketing campaigns, protests, legislative changes, and prevention programming, SV at PSIs continues (Zapp et al., 2021).

Securitisation of campus

Increasing campus security measures such as fence boundaries, improved lighting, security checks at campus entrances, high ratios of security/patrol officers to students, and off-campus safe-walk programmes have not been shown to reduce incidents of sexual assault, nor does it address the systemic causal factors that sustain SV (Cass, 2007; Quinlan, 2017; Gray & Pin, 2017). Furthermore, the emphasis on increasing campus security measures and policing demonstrates institutional investments prioritising the university's interests and reputation over the students' safety (Colpitts, 2019; Gray & Pin, 2017).

Effective sexual consent education campaigns across North America aim to create change by challenging societal norms, organisational practices, community attitudes, and behaviours of potential offenders in efforts to end SV (Haskell, 2011). In the USA, former President Obama and Vice President Biden launched the *It's On Us* campaign that used public service announcements featuring celebrities to encourage the public to take an active role in preventing campus SV (Colpitts, 2019; Sheehy & Gilbert, 2017). In Canada, one of the most common themes of prevention and education within PSIs is sexual consent, with social marketing campaigns being especially popular (Colpitts, 2019).

Since its formation in 1981, the Canadian Federation of Students (CFS) have urged PSIs to develop clear policies and processes to address SV on campuses (CFS – Ontario, 2018; Colpitts, 2019). The CFS initiated the *No Means No* campaign in the early 1990s to raise awareness and reduce the occurrence of sexual assault, acquaintance rape, and dating violence (CFS – Ontario, 2018; Colpitts, 2019; Quinlan, 2017). This popular campaign was met with some backlash in 2007 when the clothier Bluenotes Inc. started selling T-shirts in their stores across Canada with the slogan "NO MEANS have aNOther drink" (CFS – Ontario, 2018, para. 3).

Over time, the campaign shifted its language from *No Means No* to *Consent is Sexy* (Colpitts, 2019). *Consent is Sexy* is a campaign incorporating sex-positive messages to promote consent and increase sexual communication among post-secondary students (Hovick & Silver, 2019). This programme creates awareness of sexual rights and sexual communication to set boundaries (Consent is Sexy, 2011; Johnson & Hoover, 2015). It adds a different perspective of consent that addresses issues of GBV from a proactive (rather than reactive) approach (Dobson, 2012). But the language and concepts of *Consent is Sexy* campaigns have been criticised, and author and sex educator Rachel Kramer Bussel (2008) questions the integrity of the campaign, stating:

> Consent should be a baseline, the rock bottom standard for sexual activity, and shouldn't necessarily have to be sold as 'sexy' to count as something vital and important. It can be sexy, sure. But tagging it as such almost seems to be overhyping it. Do we really need to 'sell' consent as a concept?
>
> (p. 48)

Another shift in language occurred, and the CFS campaign slogan changed from *Consent is Sexy* to *Consent is Mandatory* (Colpitts, 2019). This shift corresponded to Canada's changing legal definition of consent toward an affirmative understanding of consent where "only yes means yes" (Colpitts, 2019; Gotell, 2008). Campuses across Canada have instituted *Only Yes Means Yes* campaigns to change how we view and understand sexual consent and encourage clear communication and enthusiastic consent between sexual partners (CASASC, 2021; Profitt & Ross, 2017). But these campaigns operate from the assumption that individuals have the freedom and autonomy to say no (or yes) and ignore how power and rape culture inform SV on campuses (Colpitts, 2019; Francis & Giesbrecht, 2016; Profitt & Ross, 2017)

Sexual consent educational campaigns can empower individuals to speak out against rape culture (Humphreys & Towl, 2020), as demonstrated by the York University Graduate Women's Studies Student Association (GWSSA), which began a guerrilla postering campaign crossing out the phrase *Don't get raped* with *Don't Rape*, rhetorically redirecting the responsibility away from survivors and on to the perpetrators (Ikeda & Rosser, 2010; Trusolino, 2017). Sexual consent campaigns must go beyond legal definitions of consent to tackle cultural and institutional beliefs and practices that foment and legitimise SV (Profitt & Ross, 2017). A notable example of this would be Ryerson's (now Toronto Metropolitan University) *Consent Comes First* campaign, which provides intersectional, politicised sexual consent education to students (Colpitts, 2019).

More considerable campaign work has been developed into training and programmes. Training that is linked with campaigns has been shown to have a lasting impact on students because it reinforces the messages learned in a course and helps move from a one-off dose to seeing a recurring message (Humphreys & Towl, 2020). Bystander public education campaigns and programmes (e.g., *Bringing in the Bystander*) provide opportunities to build skills for helping directly or indirectly without placing bystanders' safety in jeopardy by focusing on practising intervention strategies (Haskell, 2011).

Bystander intervention programs

Bystander education represents a recent paradigm shift in SV prevention, and bystander intervention programs (BIPs) have gained popularity as an effective CSA prevention strategy (Basile et al., 2016; Flood, 2011; Haskell, 2011; Lonsway et al., 2009). BIPs aim to establish a community of responsibility by training participants to recognise potential situations for SV and how to intervene safely (Haskell, 2011; Martell Consulting Services Ltd., 2014). But intervening is not the default for everyone. One study in Canada revealed that 90% of students who witnessed unwanted sexualised behaviour in a post-secondary setting did not act in at least one instance (Burczycka, 2020). In the same study, the students who experienced SV indicated that other people were around when it happened (Burczycka, 2020). This was the case for 60% of female students and 65% of male students who had experienced at least one incident of unwanted sexual touching, and for 31% of women and 42% of men who experienced sexual activity to which they were unable to consent because they were intoxicated, drug, manipulated, or forced in another non-physical way (Burczycka, 2020).

Although BIPs teach participants how to intervene when an act of SV is happening, they also guide how to assist people and teach skills to support a friend or loved one who discloses victimisation (Lonsway et al., 2009; Mazar, 2019). BIPs instruct participants on how to intervene proactively by challenging friends and acquaintances who perpetuate myths and stereotypes and express sexist and toxic attitudes (Lonsway et al., 2009; Mazar, 2019). The overall messaging of BIPs is to instil students with confidence and capacity to intervene responsibly and safely (Forrest & Senn, 2017; Martell Consulting Services Ltd., 2014). And the over-arching goal of engaging bystanders is to have a lasting effect on changing social norms (Haskell, 2011).

These programmes are informed by a cognitive model for bystander intervention originally outlined by Latané and Darley (1989) (Leone et al., 2018; Zapp et al., 2021) that includes five steps:

  Step 1: Observe the event.
  Step 2: Identify the situation as a potential for SV.

Step 3: Decide to intervene.
Step 4: Determine how to intervene (known as the 5Ds: direct, delegate, delay, distract, and document).
Step 5: Intervene safely.

These decision-making steps do not necessarily follow a linear path, wherein each step is subsequently achieved (Banyard, 2011, Leone et al., 2018), and people should not be shamed for choosing not to intervene. Personal circumstances and/or barriers can impact a person's choice to intervene in any of the bystander intervention steps (Leone et al., 2018).

The most crucial barrier that hinders bystander intervention is the failure to notice whether an interaction is harmful or potentially harmful and to identify the situation as a risk. Bystanders may fail to notice dangerous behaviours for numerous reasons (e.g., intoxication, sensory distractions), or it could be from subscribing to myths and stereotypes (Burn, 2008; Corboz et al., 2015). Hoxmeier et al. (2016) surveyed undergraduate students about their bystander behaviours, and students reported being less likely to see those intoxicated as victims of sexual assault (Thiessen et al., 2021).

In a Canadian study by Burczycka (2020), the most cited reason students did not act when they witnessed unwanted sexualised behaviours was that they did not see the behaviour as severe enough to warrant intervention. In the same study, some students voiced that it was not their responsibility to act and did nothing. Of all women who chose not to act, almost half (48%) stated they felt uncomfortable, were worried that there could be negative consequences (28%) or feared for their safety (18%) (Burczycka, 2020). As potential risky situations can evoke distress in bystanders, anxiety about how to help and the potential for adverse consequences can inhibit bystanders (Yule & Grych, 2020).

A bystander's affiliation with the perpetrator or victim can prevent them from intervening (Corboz et al., 2015). In the context of PSIs, the chances are that bystanders will know the participants. Fear of damaging a relationship or friendship was found to influence a person's decision not to intervene (Corboz et al., 2015; Exner-Cortens & Cummings, 2021), but overall, bystanders reported a more empathic concern and a greater personal responsibility to help their friends rather than strangers (Corboz et al., 2015; Katz et al., 2014). Perceived peer norms are influential in shaping behaviour (Johnson & Hoover, 2015). BIPs that use peer educators may be especially effective in increasing healthy sexual consent attitudes, intentions, and behaviours (Richmond & Peterson, 2020).

A study by Senn and Forrest (2016) evaluated the effectiveness of bystander intervention education with peer educators. It was found that peer educator-led workshops positively improved students' confidence, readiness, and capacity to act as prosocial bystanders for friends and strangers. Based on this finding, PSIs may consider utilising peer educators to frame SV as a shared responsibility (McMahon et al., 2013; Ruehl, n.d.). Research shows that BIPs have succeeded in increasing student engagement and supporting students, faculty, staff, and administration to intervene (Banyard et al., 2004; Forrest & Senn, 2017; Mazar, 2019), but there are some identified limitations. Social norms can hinder bystander interventions, and SV is often committed in isolation (Mazar, 2019), especially during the COVID-19 pandemic. Traditionally, prevention education has been offered outside class time to students who volunteer or seek such training. The literature outlines that this delivery method can create numerous challenges. For BIPs to be the most effective in reducing and preventing SV at PSIs, regular, consistent, and mandatory programme delivery may work better (Forrest & Senn, 2017).

Delivery mode of consent education

Sexual consent education is critical for higher education institutions to ensure that all students possess basic knowledge of key concepts, available resources, and prevention strategies (Zapp et al., 2021). Across Canada, available sexual consent education programming at PSIs is offered ad hoc and usually in person (see Chapter 4). If the COVID-19 global pandemic taught PSIs anything, it was that delivering education online is possible and sometimes preferred by students (and teachers too). Students may choose in-person or online sexual consent education based on their learning styles or personal experience with SV or related issues (Humphreys & Towl, 2020), and there are numerous factors to consider when determining the best method of delivery as summarised in the pro and cons list (Table 3.1).

In-person delivery

The most beneficial factor of in-person delivery of SV prevention programmes is that it enables engagement. Participants are more likely to engage in the training fully and are less likely to ignore large portions of content (Humphreys & Towl, 2020). In-person training is more interactive and can incorporate group work to build a sense of community and shared responsibility among student participants (Anderson & Whiston, 2005; Kleinsasser et al., 2015). A qualified facilitator benefits participants who have questions, need clarification, or need support and referrals. Skilled facilitators can be flexible and adaptive to the group's needs and can diffuse disruptions from antagonising participants when needed (Humphreys & Towl, 2020; Rockbrand & Compton, 2019).

Table 3.1 Pros and cons of in-person and online delivery of consent education.

	In-Person Delivery	*Online Delivery*
Pros	• Student engagement can be evaluated. • Training can be more interactive. • Facilitators can adapt to the audience and address negative perceptions of content. • Facilitator is present to answer questions and provide support or referrals if needed.	• Availability. • Scalability – wide dissemination. • Accessibility – closed captioning, reading-assistance. • Reliability – Delivery can be standardised. • Cost-efficiency. • Portable. • Students can remain anonymous. • Not dependent on qualified facilitators.
Cons	• Engagement and participation are not guaranteed. • Subject matter may make students feel uncomfortable discussing in the presence of others. • Delivery availability is limited due to accommodating large groups of students. • Scheduling likely to be inflexible. • Outcomes are greatly dependent on the quality of the facilitator. • Higher associated costs and resource intensive in time dedicated and materials needed.	• Evaluating student engagement not as robust. • Limited ability to use multiple training methods to engage different learning styles. • Training is less interactive (no option for group work). • Limited options for addressing questions.

Source: Authors.

Engagement from students is not guaranteed with in-person delivery of SV prevention programmes as some students may feel uncomfortable participating in discussions on this sensitive subject in the presence of others or a mixed-gender group (Humphreys & Towl, 2020; Kleinsasser et al., 2015). Students may also feel intimidated to ask for clarifications on content depending on the size of the group and the peer norms that have already been established. Sexual consent education is best conducted in a small-group format which is not ideal for reaching entire campus communities (Kleinsasser et al., 2015) and scheduling in-person training for large groups of students can take weeks, if not months on larger campuses (Humphreys & Towl, 2020; Kleinsasser et al., 2015).

Institutions must invest considerable time and resources in training and maintaining the staff necessary to implement in-person programming (Kleinsasser et al., 2015). The quality and effectiveness of this education can be impacted by the facilitator's skills, abilities, and competence (Humphreys & Towl, 2020). Delivery by various facilitators (e.g., peers, graduate students, and professionals) increases the risk of varying messaging and content. The budgets at many PSIs are constrained, SV support offices and staff are restrained and overworked, and the costs associated with in-person training are high and resource intensive (Humphreys & Towl, 2020).

Online delivery

Institutions should consider online delivery of sexual consent education because of its availability, scalability, and cost-efficiency compared to other approaches (Zapp et al., 2021). Online delivery can be made available and disseminated widely (Humphreys & Towl, 2020; Kleinsasser et al., 2015). It can be accessible to students with various disabilities, and modules could be offered in multiple languages and include closed captioning. An online consent module would promote consistency and standardised delivery (Zapp et al., 2021) and not depend on qualified facilitators. An additional bonus of online education is that it is much more cost effective than ad hoc and in-person training.

Some participants may prefer to engage in an online course to remain anonymous (Humphreys & Towl, 2020). Students can complete the training at their own pace and take breaks as needed (Englander et al., 2016; Humphreys & Towl, 2020). An online programme could also include live links to resources and counselling supports that users could access when they need them (vs. in person, where many campus counselling services are not open 24/7). The online module could connect users to support if they get triggered or to campus counsellors who could accommodate alternate delivery.

Another benefit of online interventions is that they tend to be briefer than in-person education; in fact, results of a meta-analysis indicate that shorter online interventions produce more significant effects (Cugelman et al., 2011; Kleinsasser et al., 2015). Online programming can be monitored and evaluated. Campus administrators can utilise participation tracking to monitor student progress, ensure that learners complete the course, and enforce any mandates. Programme features could also include built-in tools to collect evaluation data (RAINN, 2020; Zapp et al., 2021).

Drawbacks of online education delivery include a lack of monitoring, as there is no way of distinguishing whether a student is actively engaging with the material, just clicking through slides, or skipping to an end of course (Humphreys & Towl, 2020; Rockbrand & Compton, 2019). Online delivery is less flexible in its ability to use multiple training methods to engage different learning styles and is not as interactive as in-person programmes (Humphreys & Towl, 2020). Without a facilitator, there are more limited options for students with follow-up questions or needed clarifications (Humphreys & Towl, 2020). And if participants disagree with the content, there is no opportunity for facilitators to challenge negative beliefs and provoke thoughtful discussion (Humphreys & Towl, 2020). Research suggests that SV prevention programmes can be effectively adapted to an online format Kleinsasser et al. (2015). In a study by Mårtensson et al. (2011), participants were strongly critical of online modules, but acknowledged that quick, electronic access to resources of this sort would be extremely beneficial (Marquis et al., 2016). With the focus in higher education on the importance of graduate attributes and the increasing number of teaching and learning activities being delivered via technology, online information literacy modules have been identified as an effective way of delivering information literacy and information technology skills to students.

Overall, sexual consent education has been criticised as being limited in effectiveness because they are typically short, one-time information sessions conducted with first-year university students during initial orientation, which have little long-term impact on behaviour (Camp et al., 2018; MacDougall et al., 2020; Ortiz & Shafer, 2018). Whether delivered in-person or online, these programmes are only one piece of a comprehensive and ongoing approach to reducing levels of SV in PSIs (Zapp et al., 2021). One-time-only prevention methods are not sufficient and "booster shots" of prevention programming are needed (Quam, 2017).

Recent studies suggest that the most effective prevention programming utilises two approaches (e.g., BIPs and sexual consent education) that are generally mandated and produce strong outcomes (Berkowitz, 2016; Gidycz et al., 2011; Salazar et al., 2014; Wasco, 2015; Zapp et al., 2021). SV specialists and advocates offer such programming at PSIs, and sometimes it's mandatory or required of student athletes, residence advisors, or student council executives.

The question remains whether sexual consent education should be mandated in all Canadian PSIs, and if so, for whom?

Mandating education

The purpose of implementing sexual consent education in PSIs is to provide a safe learning space for students (Quonoey et al., 2022). In a handful of provinces, legislation dictates that PSIs must offer SV and consent education training. A smaller handful of PSIs provides mandatory in-person and online sexual consent education (see Chapter 4). A multitude of literature exists debating the efficacy and limitations of mandatory education for students and employees. Still, for years, many PSIs have felt the benefits outweigh any limitations since they mandate other training such as academic integrity, first aid, code of conduct, or cybersecurity awareness. Students are expected to read and understand their codes of student academic and non-academic conduct. Employees are expected to read and understand various policies such as conduct, academic integrity, financial processes, and evaluation. Course completion is often a prerequisite for essential integration services, such as access to housing or the ability to register for courses (RAINN, 2020). Why can't we mandate sexual violence and consent education training if we can mandate other types of training?

Compulsory training about sensitive subjects can yield high resistance from students (Marquis et al., 2016; Quonoey et al., 2022). Dobbin and Kalev (2018) suggested that mandatory training makes people feel like their behaviour is being controlled by an external power and that this feature may cause them to think that their commitment to training is being coerced (Quonoey et al., 2022). In the past, non-mandatory training has been regarded with less importance than mandatory training (Quonoey et al., 2022; Sutha et al., 2016). However, it is often better received and has a greater impact on learning outcomes (Quonoey et al., 2022; Renaud et al., 2004).

In contrast, one study argues that training is primarily successful when made mandatory (Olaniyan & Ojo, 2008) and that the compulsory nature is what makes it effective (Quonoey et al., 2022). However, it is noted that in absence of mandatory training, many people on campus would not take up available opportunities (Marquis et al., 2016).

A promotion for mandatory training and education is that it ensures the entire campus community is on the same page when it comes to consent. Mandatory sexual consent education can send a strong message that communicates the seriousness of SV and the PSI's commitment to changing the existing culture on campus (Quonoey et al., 2022; Sutha et al., 2016). There can be no excuses that someone did not know what was expected of them and the consequences should they violate a policy. Mandatory cybersecurity training, for example, ensures that all computer users do their best to prevent spam and viruses from infiltrating PSI's technology systems. It encourages everyone to work together to protect the technology and emphasises that everyone has a responsibility for technology safety.

When to engage

The literature acknowledges that SV prevention education should be provided to students as early as possible. It has been suggested that mandatory training should begin during orientation weeks or within *the red zone* (Heenehan, 2019; SVPC, 2017; University of Alberta, 2016). First-year and transfer students would benefit significantly from a mandatory and comprehensive sexual consent education available online before classes start so they are aware of the behaviour expectations and student safety support in place (Heenehan, 2019; Humphreys & Towl, 2020).

Such an orientation would provide a comprehensive and mandatory consent education for first-year and transfer students, for those residing in on-campus housing which would set the stage for education and awareness. Orientation could extend inside residence halls, cafeterias, wellness, and health centres where programming could focus on healthy sexual relationships (Heenehan, 2019).

Who to engage

It's not only students who have a high prevalence of rape myth acceptance, but also faculty and policymakers as well, therefore mandatory training should also include faculty, staff, and administrators (Heenehan, 2019). Online education and awareness-raising modules about SV can be made available to the entire campus community and be promoted widely (University of Alberta, 2016). Having an entire campus educated and informed will work towards a #cultureofconsent so that when students seek help from an employee, the faculty or staff person will know how to respond and where to direct students to resources and support. By legislating training and education programming, governments demonstrate support for campuses. Training should include programming for faculty, staff, and administration on how to respond to disclosures of sexualised violence to ensure that victims/survivors are supported in a way that prevents retraumatisation (CFS – Nova Scotia, 2017). Furthermore, campus administrators are policymakers and better policies will be created if those creators are trauma-informed and educated about the systems that sustain SV.

Conclusion

Sexual consent is contextual and can be convoluted. Within the context of Canadian PSIs, factors such as rape culture, stereotypes, myths, cultural norms, media, legislation, and social-cultural aspects all influence how students understand, accept, and practise sexual consent. The absence of consent is a key feature of SV, and the literature illustrates that students have a wavy understanding of consent and there is much confusion and debate about what constitutes consensual sexual behaviour. The language of consent and sexual communication used by students is informed by sexual scripts and gender roles that do not always follow conventional standards. Sexual consent education creates awareness and informs students (as well as faculty and staff) of the statistical realities of SV on Canadian campuses and how to use consent in their interactions. What PSIs do matters, and previous efforts to provide fulsome prevention, education, and intervention responses have fallen short as evidenced by the continued prevalence of SV within campus communities.

References

Adams-Curtis, L. E., & Forbes, G. B. (2004). College women's experiences of sexual coercion: A review of cultural, perpetrator, victim, and situational variables. *Trauma, Violence, & Abuse, 5*(2), 91–122. https://journals.sagepub.com/doi/epdf/10.1177/1524838003262331

Ahmed, S. (2017). *Living a feminist life.* Duke University Press.

Allen, C. (2011, September 19). *The feminist war on fraternities.* www.mindingthecampus.org/2011/09/19/the_feminist_war_on_fraterniti/

Anderson, E. (2022). A phenomenological approach to sexual consent. *Feminist Philosophy Quarterly, 8*(2), 1–25. https://ojs.lib.uwo.ca/index.php/fpq/index

Anderson, L. A., & Whiston, S. C. (2005). Sexual assault education programs: A meta-analytic examination of their effectiveness. *Psychology of Women Quarterly, 29*(4), 374–388. https://journals.sagepub.com/doi/epub/10.1111/j.1471-6402.2005.00237.x

Armstrong, E. A., Hamilton, L., & Sweeney, B. (2006). Sexual assault on campus: A multilevel, integrative approach to party rape. *Social Problems, 53*(4), 483–499. https://doi.org/10.1525/sp.2006.53.4.483

Bannon, R. S., Brosi, M. W., & Foubert, J. D. (2013). Sorority women's and fraternity men's rape myth acceptance and bystander intervention attitudes. *Journal of Student Affairs Research and Practice, 50*(1), 72–87. https://doi.org/10.1515/jsarp-2013-0005

Banyard, V. L. (2011). Who will help prevent sexual violence: Creating an ecological model of bystander intervention. *Psychology of Violence, 1*, 216–229. http://dx.doi.org/10.1037/a0023739

Banyard, V. L., Plante, E. G., & Moynihan, M. M. (2004). Bystander education: Bringing a broader community perspective to sexual violence prevention. *Journal of Community Psychology, 32*, 61–79. http://dx.doi.org/10.1002/jcop.10078

Basile, K. C., DeGue, S., Jones, K., Freire, K., Dills, J., Smith, S. G., & Raiford, J. L. (2016). *Stop SV: A technical package to prevent sexual violence.* www.cdc.gov/violenceprevention/pdf/SV-Prevention-Technical-Package.pdf

Benoit, A. A., & Ronis, S. T. (2022). A qualitative examination of withdrawing sexual consent, sexual compliance, and young women's role as sexual gatekeepers. *International Journal of Sexual Health*, 1–16. https://doi.org/10.1080/19317611.2022.2089312

Beres, M. A. (2007). "spontaneous" sexual consent: An analysis of sexual consent literature. *Feminism & Psychology, 17*(1), 93–108. https://doi.org/10.1177/0959353507072914

Beres, M. A. (2014). Rethinking the concept of consent for anti-sexual violence activism and education. *Feminism & Psychology, 24*(3), 373–389. https://journals.sagepub.com/doi/epub/10.1177/0959353514539652

Beres, M. (2020). Perspectives of rape-prevention educators on the role of consent in sexual violence prevention. *Sex Education*, *20*(2), 227–238. https://doi.org/10. 1080/14681811.2019.1621744

Berkowitz, A. D. (2016). *Integrating social norms approach and bystander intervention in sexual assault and AOD prevention.* www.alanberkowitz.com

Boswell, A. A., & Spade, J. Z. (1996). Fraternities and collegiate rape culture: Why are some fraternities more dangerous places for women? *Gender & Society*, *10*(2), 133–147. http://dx.doi.org/10.1177/089124396010002003

Bourassa, C., Bendig, M., Oleson, E. J., Ozog, C. A., Billan, J. L., Owl, N., & Ross-Hopley, L. (2017). Campus violence, Indigenous women, and the policy void. In E. Quinlan, A. Quinlan, C. Fogel, & G. Taylor (Eds.), *Sexual violence at Canadian universities: Activism, institutional responses, and strategies for change* (pp. 45–59). ProQuest Ebook Central. https://ebookcentral.proquest.com

Brady, G., Lowe, P., Brown, G., Osmond, J., & Newman, M. (2018). "All in all it is just a judgement call": Issues surrounding sexual consent in young people's heterosexual encounters. *Journal of Youth Studies*, *21*(1), 35–50. https://doi.org/1 0.1080/13676261.2017.1343461

Burczycka, M. (2020). *Students' experiences of unwanted sexualized behaviours and sexual assault at postsecondary schools in the Canadian provinces, 2019.* Canadian Centre for Justice and Community Safety Statistics. https://www150. statcan.gc.ca/n1/pub/85-002-x/2020001/article/00005-eng.htm

Burn, S. M. (2008). A situational model of sexual assault prevention through bystander intervention. *Sex Roles*, *60*(11–12), 779–792. https://doi.org/10.1007/ s11199-008-9581-5

Bussel, R. K. (2008). Beyond yes or no: Consent as sexual process. In J. Friedman & J. Valenti (Eds.), *Yes means yes! Visions of female sexual power & a world without rape* (pp. 43–53). Seal Press. http://challengingmalesupremacy.org/wp-content/uploads/2015/03/Beyond-Yes-or-No-Consent-as-Sexual-Process.pdf

Byers, E. S. (1996). How well does the traditional sexual script explain sexual coercion? Review of a program of research. *Journal of Psychology & Human Sexuality*, *8*(1–2), 7–25. http://dx.doi.org/10.1300/J056v08n01_02

Cahill, A. J. (2017). Why theory matters: Using philosophical resources to develop university practices and policies regarding sexual violence. In E. Quinlan, A. Quinlan, C. Fogel, & G. Taylor (Eds.), *Sexual violence at Canadian universities: Activism, institutional responses, and strategies for change* (pp. 275–289). ProQuest Ebook Central. https://ebookcentral.proquest.com

Camp, S. J., Sherlock-Smith, A. C., & Davies, E. L. (2018). Awareness and support: Students' views about the prevention of sexual assault on UK campuses. *Health Education*, *118*(5), 431–446. https://doi.org/10.1108/HE-02-2018-0007

Canadian Federation of Students. (2018). *Gender-based violence.* https://cfsontario. ca/campaigns/gender-based-violence/

Canadian Federation of Students – Ontario (CFS – Ontario). (2015, December). *Fact sheet: Sexual violence on campus.* https://cfsontario.ca/wpcontent/ uploads/2017/07/Factsheet-SexualAssault.pdf

Canadian Intergovernmental Conference Secretariat (CICS). (2018). *Reporting, investigating and prosecuting sexual assaults committed against adults –*

Challenges and promising practices in enhancing access to justice for victims –
CICS/SCIC. https://scics.ca/en/product-produit/reporting-investigating-and-pros-
ecuting-sexual-assaults-committed-against-adults-challenges-and-promising-
practices-in-enhancing-access-to-justice-for-victims/#fn23-rf

Canadian Women's Foundation. (2015, May 5). *Only 1 in 3 Canadians know what*
sexual consent means. https://canadianwomen.org/about-us/media/1-3-canadians-
know-sexual-consent-means/

Canadian Women's Foundation. (2018, May 16). *Survey finds drop in Canadians'*
understanding of consent. https://canadianwomen.org/survey-finds-drop-in-
canadians-understanding-of-consent/

Cass, A. (2007). Routine activities and sexual assault: An analysis of individual –
and school-level factors. *Violence and Victims, 22*(3), 350–364. https://doi.org/
10.1891/088667007780842810

CBC News. (2013, September 7). *UBC investigates frosh students' pro-rape chant.*
www.cbc.ca/news/canada/british-columbia/ubc-investigates-frosh-students-pro-
rape-chant-1.1699589

CCI Research Inc. (2019, March 19). *Student voices on sexual violence: Summary*
report of the student voices on sexual violence survey. https://files.ontario.ca/tcu-
summary-report-student-voices-on-sexual-violence-survey-en-2019-03.pdf

Center for Substance Abuse Treatment. (2014). Understanding the impact of trauma.
Trauma-informed care in behavioral health services, No. 57. Chapter 3, Understanding the Impact of Trauma. www.ncbi.nlm.nih.gov/books/NBK207191/

Central Alberta Sexual Assault Support Centre. (2021, November 4). *Only yes*
means yes when it comes to consent. https://casasc.ca/only-yes-means-yes-when-
it-comes-to-consent/

Colpitts, E. M. (2019). *An intersectional analysis of sexual violence policies,*
responses, and prevention efforts at Ontario universities (Dissertation). https://
yorkspace.library.yorku.ca/xmlui/handle/10315/36778

Conroy, S., & Cotter, A. (2017). Self-reported sexual assault in Canada, 2014. *Juri-*
stat (Statistics Canada Catalogue no. 85-002-X). https://www150.statcan.gc.ca/
n1/en/pub/85-002-x/2017001/article/14842-eng.pdf?st=9A3jjLTw

Consent is Sexy. (2011). *About consent is sexy campaign: Frequently asked ques-*
tions. www.consentissexy.net/about-faqs

Corboz, J., Flood, M., & Dyson, S. (2015). Challenges of bystander intervention in
male-dominated professional sport: Lessons from the Australian football league.
Violence Against Women, 22(3), 1–20. https://doi.org/10.1177/1077801215602343

Cotter, A. (2021, August 25). Criminal victimization in Canada, 2019. *Juristat* (Statistics Canada Catalogue no. 85-002-X). https://www150.statcan.gc.ca/n1/en/
pub/85-002-x/2021001/article/00014-eng.pdf?st=j_yLxP5q

Coubrough, J. (2018, March 9). More survivors coming forward to report sex
assaults after #Metoo movement. *CBC News.* www.cbc.ca/news/canada/manitoba/
winnipeg-police-sexual-assault-reports-up-metoo-1.4568787

Council of Ontario Universities. (2020). *Student voices on sexual violence: Overview*
of selected survey results from the university sector. https://ontariouniversities.ca/

wp-content/uploads/2020/02/COU-Student-Voices-Survey-Results_Overview-Feb-27-2020-FINAL.pdf

Cugelman, B., Thelwall, M., & Dawes, P. (2011). Online interventions for social marketing health behavior change campaigns: A meta-analysis of psychological architectures and adherence factors. *Journal of Medical Internet Research, 13*(1), 17. https://doi.org/10.2196/jmir.1367

Curtis, J. N., & Burnett, S. (2017). Affirmative consent: What do college student leaders think about "yes means yes" as the standard for sexual behavior? *American Journal of Sexuality Education, 12*(3), 201–214. https://doi.org/10.1080/15546128.2017.1328322

Cusmano, D. (2018). Rape culture rooted in patriarchy, media portrayal, and victim blaming. *Writing Across the Curriculum, 30*. https://digitalcommons.sacredheart.edu/wac_prize/30

DeKeseredy, W. S., Schwartz, M. D., & Tait, K. (1993). Sexual assault and stranger aggression on a Canadian university campus. *Sex Roles: A Journal of Research, 28*(5–6), 263–277. https://doi.org/10.1007/BF00289885

Deming, M. E., Covan, E. K., Swan, S. C., & Billings, D. L. (2013). Exploring rape myths, gendered norms, group processing, and the social context of rape among college women: A qualitative analysis. *Violence against Women, 19*(4), 465–465. https://doi.org/10.1177/1077801213487044

Dixie, K. D. (2017). Defining consent as a factor in sexual assault prevention. *McNair Scholars Research Journal, 10*(1), Article 5. http://commons.emich.edu/mcnair/vol10/iss1/5

Dobbin, F., & Kalev, A. (2018). Why doesn't diversity training work? The challenge for industry and academia. *Anthropology Now, 10*(2), 48–55. https://doi.org/10.1080/19428200.2018.1493182

Dobson, H. (2012, September 19). Opinion: Consent is sexy takes a "different approach" to gender-based violence. *The Charlatan*. https://charlatan.ca/2012/09/19/opinion-consent-is-sexy-takes-a-different-approach-to-gender-based-violence/

Edwards, K., Turchik, J., Dardis, C., Reynolds, N., & Gidycz, C. (2011). Rape myths: History, individual and institutional-level presence, and implications for change. *Sex Roles, 65*(11–12), 761–773. https://doi.org/10.1007/s11199-011-9943-2

Englander, E., Mccoy, M., & Sherman, S. (2016). Sexual assault information on university websites. *Violence and Gender, 3*(1), 64–70. https://doi.org/10.1089/vio.2015.0025

Exner-Cortens, D., & Cummings, N. (2021). Bystander-based sexual violence prevention with college athletes: A pilot randomized trial. *Journal of Interpersonal Violence, 36*(1–2), 211. https://doi.org/10.1177/0886260517733279

Fenner, L. (2017). Sexual consent as a scientific subject: A literature review. *American Journal of Sexuality Education, 12*(4), 451–471. https://doi.org/10.1080/15546128.2017.1393646

Filipovic, J. (2008). Offensive feminism: The conservative gender norms that perpetuate rape culture, and how feminists can fight back. In *Yes means yes: Visions of female sexual power & a world without rape* (pp. 13–27). Seal Press. http://

theconsentworkshop.com/wpcontent/uploads/2019/02/Jaclyn-Friedman-Jessica-Valenti-Yes-Means-Yes_-Visions-of-Female-Sexual-Power-and-A-World-Without-Rape-2008-Seal-Press.pdf

Flood, M. (2011). Involving men in efforts to end violence against women. *Men and Masculinities, 14*(3), 358–377. https://doi.org/10.1177/1097184X10363995

Forrest, A., & Senn, C. Y. (2017). Theory becomes practice: The bystander initiative at the University of Windsor. In E. Quinlan, A. Quinlan, C. Fogel, & G. Taylor (Eds.), *Sexual violence at Canadian universities: Activism, institutional responses, and strategies for change* (pp. 175–192). ProQuest Ebook Central. https://ebookcentral.proquest.com

Francis, M., & Giesbrecht, J. (2016). *From the margins to the centre: Re-thinking sexual violence education and support at Brock University.* https://dr.library.brocku.ca/handle/10464/12729

The Fulcrum. (2018, November 14). *The "red zone".* https://thefulcrum.ca/features/the-red-zone/

Gagnon, J. H., & Simon, W. (1973). Sexual conduct: The social sources of human sexuality. *The Sociological Quarter, 16*(1), 135–139. www.jstor.org/stable/pdf/4105542.pdf

Garcia, C., & Vemuri, A. (2017). Theorizing "rape culture": How law, policy, and education can support and end sexual violence. *Education & Law Journal, 27*(1), 1–17. www.proquest.com/scholarly-journals/theorizing-rape-culture-how-law-policy-education/docview/1983614241/se-2

Garcia, S. E. (2017, October 20). The woman who created #Me-Too long before hashtags. *New York Times.* www.nytimes.com/2017/10/20/us/me-too-movement-tarana-burke.html

Gidycz, C. A., Orchowski, L. M., & Berkowitz, A. D. (2011). Preventing sexual aggression among college men: An evaluation of a social norms and bystander intervention program. *Violence against Women, 17*(6), 720–720. https://doi.org/10.1177/1077801211409727

Gotell, L. (2008). Rethinking affirmative consent in Canadian sexual assault law: Neoliberal sexual subjects and risky women. *Akron Law Review, 41*(4), 865–898.

Government of Canada. (2021, July 7). *A definition of consent to sexual activity.* www.justice.gc.ca/eng/cj-jp/victims-victimes/def.html

Gray, M., & Pin, L. (2017). "I would like it if some of our tuition went to providing pepper spray for student": University branding, securitization and campus sexual assault at a Canadian University. *The Annual Review of Interdisciplinary Justice Research, 6*, 86–110. CanLIIDocs 4075. https://canlii.ca/t/t9kg

Hall, D. S. (1998). Consent for sexual behavior in a college student population. *Electronic Journal of Human Sexuality, 1.* www.ejhs.org/volume1/consent1.htm

Harris, K. L. (2018). Yes means yes and no means no, but both these mantras need to go: Communication myths in consent education and anti-rape activism. *Journal of Applied Communication Research, 46*(2). https://doi.org/10.1080/00909882.2018.1435900

Haskell, L. (2011). *Key best practices for effective sexual violence public education campaigns: A summary.* www.arts.on.ca/oac/media/oac/Community%20

Engagement%20Fund/Key-Best-Practices-for-Effective-Sexual-Violence-Public-Education-Campaigns-A-Summary-(PDF).pdf

Heenehan, F. M. (2019). Best practices in consent education: An analysis. *The Vermont Connection*, *40*(16), 115–122. https://scholarworks.uvm.edu/tvc/vol40/iss1/16

Hickman, S. E., & Muehlenhard, C. L. (1999). "By the semi-mystical appearance of a condom": How young women and men communicate sexual consent in heterosexual situations. *The Journal of Sex Research*, *36*(3), 258–272. www.jstor.org/stable/3813437

Hirsch, J. S., Khan, S. R., Wamboldt, A., & Mellins, C. A. (2018). Social dimensions of sexual consent among cisgender heterosexual college students: Insights from ethnographic research. *Society for Adolescent Health and Medicine*, *64*, 26–35. https://doi.org/10.1016/j.jadohealth.20 18.06.011

Hovick, S. R., & Silver, N. (2019). "Consent is sexy": A poster campaign using sex-positive images and messages to increase dyadic sexual communication. *Journal of American College Health*, *67*(8), 817–824. https://doi.org/10.1080/07448481.2018.1515746

Hoxmeier, J. C., Flay, B. R., & Acock, A. C. (2016). Control, norms, and attitudes: Differences between students who do and do not intervene as bystanders to sexual assault. *Journal of Interpersonal Violence*, *33*(15), 2379–2401. https://doi.org/10.1177/0886260515625503

Humphreys, C. J., & Towl, G. J. (2020). *Addressing student sexual violence in higher education: A good practice guide.* Emerald Publishing Limited.

Humphreys, T. P. (2004). Understanding sexual consent: An empirical investigation of the normative script for young heterosexual adults. *Making Sense of Sexual Consent*, 209–225. www.researchgate.net/publication/242316851

Humphreys, T. P., & Brousseau, M. M. (2010). The sexual consent scale – revised: Development, reliability, and preliminary validity. *Journal of Sex Research*, *47*(5), 420–428. https://doi.org/10.1080/00224490903151358

Hust, S. J. T., Rodgers, K. B., & Bayly, B. (2017). Scripting sexual consent: Internalized traditional sexual scripts and sexual consent expectancies among college students. *Family Relations*, *66*(1), 197–210. https://doi.org/10.1111/fare.12230

Ikeda, N., & Rosser, E. (2010). "You be vigilant! Don't rape!": Reclaiming space and security at York university. *Canadian Woman Studies*, *28*(1), 37–43. www.proquest.com/scholarly-journals/you-be-vigilant-dont-rape-reclaiming-space/docview/755499670/se-2

Jackson, A. (2018, January 28). Most sororities have to follow a sexist and potentially dangerous rule that gives men on college campuses power. *Business Insider.* www.businessinsider.com/most-sororities-cant-throw-parties-with-alcohol-2018-1

Jacobs, S. (2021, September 14). *Working together to end the red zone.* Imprint. http://uwimprint.ca/article/working-together-to-end-the-red-zone/

Jaffe, A. E., Steel, A. L., DiLillo, D., Messman-Moore, T. L., & Gratz, K. L. (2021). Characterizing sexual violence in intimate relationships: An examination of blame attributions and rape acknowledgment. *Journal of Interpersonal Violence*, *36*(1–2), 469–490. https://doi.org/10.1177/0886260517726972

Johnson, A. M., & Hoover, S. M. (2015). The potential of sexual consent interventions on college campuses: A literature review on the barriers to establishing affirmative sexual consent. *PURE Insights*, *4*(5). http://digitalcommons.wou.edu/pure/vol4/iss1/5

Jozkowski, K. N. (2013). The influence of consent on college students' perceptions of the quality of sexual intercourse at last event. *International Journal of Sexual Health*, *25*(4), 260–272. https://doi.org/10.1080/19317611.2013.799626

Jozkowski, K. N., & Peterson, Z. (2013). College students and sexual consent: Unique insights. *The Journal of Sex Research*, *50*(6), 517–523. https://doi.org/10.1080/00224499.2012.700739

Jozkowski, K. N., Peterson, Z., Sanders, S., Dennis, B., & Reece, M. (2014). Gender differences in heterosexual college students' conceptualizations and indicators of sexual consent: Implications for contemporary sexual assault prevention education. *The Journal of Sex Research*, *51*(8), 904–916. https://doi.org/10.1080/00224499.2013.792326

Jozkowski, K. N., & Wiersma, J. D. (2015). Does drinking alcohol prior to sexual activity influence college students' consent? *International Journal of Sexual Health*, *27*(2), 156–174. https://doi.org/10.1080/19317611.2014.951505

Katz, J., & Moore, J. (2013). Bystander education training for campus sexual assault prevention: An initial meta-analysis. *Violence and Victims*, *28*(6), 1054–1067. http://doi.org/10.1891/0886-6708.VV-D-12-00113

Katz, J., Pazienza, R., Olin, R., & Rich, H. (2014). That's what friends are for: Bystander responses to friends or strangers at risk for party rape victimization. *Journal of Interpersonal Violence*, *30*(16), 2775–2792. https://doi.org/10.1177/0886260514554290

Keighley, K. (2017, July 24). Police-reported crime statistics in Canada, 2016. *Juristat* (Statistics Canada Catalogue no. 85–002-X). https://www150.statcan.gc.ca/n1/pub/85-002-x/2017001/article/54842-eng.pdf

Kitzinger, C., & Frith, H. (1999). Just say no? The use of conversation analysis in developing a feminist perspective on sexual refusal. *Discourse and Society*, *10*(3), 293–316. https://doi.org/10.1177/09579265990100030

Kleinsasser, A., Jouriles, E. N., McDonald, R., & Rosenfield, D. (2015). An online bystander intervention program for the prevention of sexual violence. *Psychol Violence*, *5*(3), 227–235. www.ncbi.nlm.nih.gov/pmc/articles/PMC4521419/pdf/nihms627641.pdf

Krahé, B., Scheinberger-Olwig, R., & Kolpin, S. (2000). Ambiguous communication of sexual intentions as a risk marker of sexual aggression. *Sex Roles*, *42*, 313–337. http://dx.doi.org/10.1023/A:1007080303569

Krause, K. H., Miedema, S. S., Woofter, R., & Yount, K. M. (2017). Feminist research with student activists: Enhancing campus sexual assault research. *Family Relations*, *66*(1), 211–223. https://doi.org/10.1111/fare.12239

Laframboise, K. (2017, October 20). Calls flood Montreal police hotline for victims of sexual misconduct. *CBC News*. www.cbc.ca/news/canada/montreal/montreal-police-calls-flooding-in-sexual-assault-quebecers-1.4364180

Lakin Afolabi Law. (2022, April 14). *What is the difference between sexual assault and rape?* https://lakinafolabilaw.com/difference-between-sexual-assault-and-rape-lakin-afolabi-law/

Lanza-Kaduce, L., Capece, M., & Alden, H. (2006). Liquor is quicker: Gender and social learning among college students. *Criminal Justice Policy Review, 17*(2), 127–143. http://dx.doi.org/10.1177/0887403405279934

Latané, B., & Darley, J. M. (1989). *The unresponsive bystander: Why doesn't he help?* Prentice Hall.

Leone, R. M., Haikalis, M., Parrott, D. J., & DiLillo, D. (2018). Bystander intervention to prevent sexual violence: The overlooked role of bystander alcohol intoxication. *Psychology of Violence, 8*(5), 639–647. http://dx.doi.org/10.1037/vio0000155

Linder, C. (2018). *Sexual violence on campus: Power-conscious approaches to awareness, prevention, and response.* Emerald Publishing Limited.

Lonsway, K. A., Banyard, V. L., Berkowitz, A. D., Gidycz, C. A., & Katz, J. T. (2009). *Rape prevention and risk reduction: Review of the research literature for practitioners.* The National Online Resource Center on Violence against Women. https://vawnet.org/material/rape-prevention-and-risk-reduction-review-research-literature-practitioners

MacDougall, A., Craig, S., Goldsmith, K., & Byers, E. S. (2020). #consent: University students' perceptions of their sexual consent education. *The Canadian Journal of Human Sexuality, 29*(2), 154–166. https://doi.org/10.3138/cjhs.2020-0007

MacKinnon, C., & Hayden, P. (2001). Rape, genocide, and women's human rights. In *The philosophy of human rights.* Paragon House.

Marquis, E., Jung, B., Fudge Schormans, A., Lukmanji, S., Wilton, R., & Baptiste, S. (2016). Developing inclusive educators: enhancing the accessibility of teaching and learning in higher education. *International Journal for Academic Development, 21*(4), 337–349. https://www.tandfonline.com/doi/epdf/10.1080/136014 4X.2016.1181071?needAccess=true&role=button

Martell Consulting Services Ltd. (2014). *Student safety in Nova Scotia: A review of student union policies and practices to prevent sexual violence.* www.studentsns. ca/s/2014-05-09-sexual-assault-report-KB-for-web1.pdf

Mårtensson, K., Roxå, T., & Olsson, T. (2011). Developing a quality culture through the scholarship of teaching and learning. *Higher Education Research & Development, 30*(1), 51–62.

Marzell, M., Bavarian, N., Paschall, M. J., Mair, C., & Saltz, R. F. (2015). Party characteristics, drinking settings, and college students' risk of intoxication: A multi-campus study. *The Journal of Primary Prevention, 36*(4), 247–258. https:// doi.org/10.1007/s10935-015-0393-4

Mazar, L. (2019). History and theoretical understanding of bystander intervention. In W. T. O'Donohue & P. A. Schewe (Eds.), *Handbook of sexual assault and sexual assault prevention* (pp. 423–432). Springer. https://doi.org/10.1007/978-3-030-23645-8

McCabe, S. (2018, September 18). The "red zone": Why early education on sexual assault is critical for universities. *The Ubyssey.* www.ubyssey.ca/news/ why-early-education-on-sexual-assault-is-critical/

McMahon, S., Hoffman, M. L., McMahon, S. M., Zucker, S., & Koenick, R. A. (2013). What would you do? Strategies for bystander intervention to prevent sexual violence by college students. *Journal of College and Character, 14*(2), 141–152. https://doi.org/10.1515/jcc-2013–0019

Mehta, S. (2018, July 25). 2017 sexual assault cases at their highest in five years. *London Free Press*. https://lfpress.com/news/local-news/2017-sexual-assault-cases-at-their-highest-in-five-years

Mendes, K., Ringrose, J., & Keller, J. (2018). #Metoo and the promise and pitfalls of challenging rape culture through digital feminist activism. *European Journal of Women's Studies, 25*(2), 236–246. https://doi.org/10.1177/1350506818765318

Moreau, G. (2019, July 22). Police-reported crime statistics in Canada, 2018. *Juristat* (Statistics Canada Catalogue no. 85–002-X). https://www150.statcan.gc.ca/n1/pub/85-002-x/2019001/article/00013-eng.htm

Moreau, G. (2022, August 3). Police-reported crime statistics in Canada, 2021. *Juristat* (Statistics Canada Catalogue no. 85–002-X). https://www150.statcan.gc.ca/n1/pub/85-002-x/2022001/article/00013-eng.pdf

Moreau, G., Jaffray, B., & Armstrong, A. (2020, October 29). Police-reported crime statistics in Canada, 2019. *Juristat* (Statistics Canada Catalogue no. 85–002-X). https://www150.statcan.gc.ca/n1/pub/85-002-x/2020001/article/00010-eng.htm

Moyano, N., Sánchez-Fuentes, M. del M., Parra-Barrera, S. M., & Granados de Haro, R. (2022). Only "yes" means "yes": Negotiation of sex and its link with sexual violence. *Journal of Interpersonal Violence, 0*(0), 1–19. https://doi.org/10.1177/08862605221102483

Muehlenhard, L. C., Humphreys, P. T., Jozkowski, N. K., & Peterson, D. Z. (2016). The complexities of sexual consent among college students: A conceptual and empirical review. *The Journal of Sex Research, 53*(4–5), 457–487. https://doi.org/10.1080/00224499.2016.1146651

Murnen, S. K., Wright, C., & Kaluzny, G. (2002). If "boys will be boys," then girls will be victims? A meta-analytic review of the research that relates masculine ideology to sexual aggression. *Sex Roles: A Journal of Research, 46*(11–12), 359–375. https://doi.org/10.1023/A:1020488928736

Newton-Taylor, B., Dewit, D., & Gliksman, L. (1998). Prevalence and factors associated with physical and sexual assault of female university students in Ontario. *Health Care for Women International, 19*(2), 155–164. https://doi.org/10.1080/073993398246485

Olaniyan, D. A., & Ojo, L. B. (2008). Staff training and development: A Vital tool for organizational effectiveness. *European Journal of Scientific Research, 24*(3), 326–331.

Orchard, T. (2021, September 19). Western University and other schools should cancel frosh week to stop rape culture. *The Conversation*. https://theconversation.com/western-university-and-other-schools-should-cancel-frosh-week-to-stop-rape-culture-167962#:~:text=Student%2Dled%20activism%20and%20ongoing,to%20happen%20during%20frosh%20week

Ortiz, R. R., & Shafer, A. (2018). Unblurring the lines of sexual consent with a college student-driven sexual consent education campaign. *Journal of American College Health, 66*(6), 450–456. https://doi.org/10.1080/07448481.2018.1431902

Ostridge, L., & O'Connor, C. D. (2020). Reporting unwanted sexual behavior at a post-secondary institution: Student understandings of campus policy. *Canadian Journal of Family and Youth*, *12*(1), 225–242. http://ejournals.library.ualberta.ca/index/php/cjfy

Patterson, D., & Campbell, R. (2010). Why rape survivors participate in the criminal justice system. *Journal of Community Psychology*, *38*(2), 191–205. www.researchgate.net/publication/230205791_Why_Rape_Survivors_Participate_in_the_Criminal_Justice_System

Perreault, S. (2015, November 23). Criminal victimization in Canada, 2014. *Juristat* (Statistics Canada Catalogue no. 85–002-X). https://www150.statcan.gc.ca/n1/pub/85-002-x/2015001/article/14241-eng.pdf

Profitt, N. J., & Ross, N. (2017). A critical analysis of the report *Student Safety in Nova Scotia*: Co-creating a vision and language for safer and socially just campus communities. In E. Quinlan, A. Quinlan, C. Fogel, & G. Taylor (Eds.), *Sexual violence at Canadian universities: Activism, institutional responses, and strategies for change* (pp. 193–218). ProQuest Ebook Central. https://ebookcentral.proquest.com

Public Health Agency of Canada. (2019). *Canadian guidelines for sexual health education*. www.canada.ca/content/dam/phac-aspc/migration/phac-aspc/publicat/cgshe-ldnemss/pdf/guidelines-eng.pdf

Quam, S. (2017). *Ending rape: Effective strategies for reducing sexual and relationship violence on a college campus*. Syracuse University Honors Program Capstone Projects. 1028. https://surface.syr.edu/honors_capstone/1028

Quinlan, E. (2017). Introduction: Sexual violence in the ivory tower. In E. Quinlan, A. Quinlan, C. Fogel, & G. Taylor (Eds.), *Sexual violence at Canadian universities: Activism, institutional responses, and strategies for change* (pp. 1–24). ProQuest Ebook Central. https://ebookcentral.proquest.com

Quonoey, J., Coombe, L., & Willis, J. (2022). Mandatory versus non-mandatory training in culturally safe practices for education staff at universities. *Alternative: An International Journal of Indigenous Peoples*, *18*(1), 19–25 https://doi.org/10.1177/11771801221087825

RAINN. (2020). *Haven – Understanding sexual assault*. https://preventionnavigator.rainn.org/program/haven/

Renaud, S., Lakhdari, M., Morin, L., & Montreuil, S. (2004). The determinants of participation in non-mandatory training. *Relations Industrielles*, *59*(4), 724–743. https://doi.org/10.7202/011336ar

Richmond, K. P., & Peterson Zoë, D. (2020). Perceived sex education and its association with consent attitudes, intentions, and communication. *American Journal of Sexuality Education*, *15*(1), 1–24. https://doi.org/10.1080/15546128.2019.1669512

Righi, M. K., Bogen, K. W., Kuo, C., & Orchowski, L. M. (2021). A qualitative analysis of beliefs about sexual consent among high school students. *Journal of Interpersonal Violence*, *36*(15–16), NP8290–NP8316. https://doi.org/10.1177/0886260519842855

Rockbrand, B., & Compton, I. (2019, October 1). It takes all of us online consent training faces backlash. *The Link*. https://thelinknewspaper.ca/article/it-takes-all-of-us-online-consent-training-faces-backlash

78   *Understanding consent education*

Rollo, T. (n.d.). *Sexual consent and sexual violence.* www.academia.edu/36891870/
Getting_to_the_Roots_of_Consent_and_Sexual_violence
Rose, S., & Frieze, I. H. (1989). Young singles' scripts for a first date. *Gender and
Society, 3*(2), 258–268. https://doi.org/10.1177/089124389003002006
Rose, S., & Frieze, I. H. (1993). Young singles' contemporary dating scripts. *Sex
Roles: A Journal of Research, 28*(9–10), 499–509. https://doi.org/10.1007/
BF00289677
Rotenberg, C., & Cotter, A. (2018, November 8). Police-reported sexual assaults in
Canada before and after #MeToo, 2016 and 2017. *Juristat* (Statistics Canada Cat-
alogue no. 85–002-X). https://www150.statcan.gc.ca/n1/pub/85-002-x/2018001/
article/54979-eng.htm
Ruehl, M. C. (n.d.). *How universities are using interactive theater to address sexual
assault: A review of literature and the way forward through mindful reflection.*
www.academia.edu/31992407/How_Universities_are_Using_Interactive_Theater_
to_Address_Sexual_Assault_A_Review_of_Literature_and_the_Way_Forward_
through_Mindful_Reflection
R. v. Ewanchuk [1999] 1 S.C.R. 330.
Salazar, L. F., Vivolo-Kantor, A., Hardin, J., & Berkowitz, A. (2014). A web-based
sexual violence bystander intervention for male college students: Randomized
controlled trial. *Journal of Medical Internet Research, 16*(9), e203. https://doi.
org/10.2196/jmir.3426
Salvino, C., Gilchrist, K., & Cooligan-Pang, J. (2017). *OurTurn: A national action
plan to end campus sexual violence.* Student's Society of McGill University.
https://static1.squarespace.com/static/5bc4e7bcf4755a6e42b00495/t/5f107ac2b2
f3cd2f9b6fe449/1594915540325/our_turn_action_plan_en_2020-05-26.pdf
Scott, K. D., & Graves, C. (2017). Sexual violence, consent, and contradictions: A
call for communication scholars to impact sexual violence prevention. *Pursuit –
The Journal of Undergraduate Research at the University of Tennessee, 8*(1),
Article 16. http://trace.tennessee.edu/pursuit/vol8/iss1/16
Senn, C. Y., Eliasziw, M., Hobden, K. L., Newby-Clark, I. R., Barata, P. C., Radtke,
H. L., & Thurston, W. E. (2017). Secondary and 2-year outcomes of a sexual
assault resistance program for university women. *Psychology of Women Quarterly, 41*(2), 147–162. https://doi.org/10.1177/0361684317690119
Senn, C. Y., & Forrest, A. (2016). "And then one night when I went to class . . . ": The
impact of sexual assault bystander intervention workshops incorporated in academic
courses. *Psychology of Violence, 6*(4), 607–618. https://doi.org/10.1037/a0039660
Sexual Violence Prevention Committee (SVPC). (2017, December 15). *Changing
the culture of acceptance: Recommendations to address sexual violence on university campuses.* Council of Nova Scotia University Presidents. https://novascotia.
ca/lae/pubs/docs/changing-the-culture-of-acceptance.pdf
Shaffer, M. (2012). The impact of the Charter on the law of sexual assault: Plus ça
change, plus c'est la même chose. *The Supreme Court Law Review: Osgoode's
Annual Constitutional Cases Conference, 57.* https://digitalcommons.osgoode.
yorku.ca/sclr/vol57/iss1/15
Sheehy, E., & Gilbert, D. (2017). Responding to sexual assault on campus: What can
Canadian universities learn from U.S. law and policy? In E. Quinlan, A. Quinlan,

C. Fogel, & G. Taylor (Eds.), *Sexual violence at Canadian universities: Activism, institutional responses, and strategies for change* (pp. 291–327). ProQuest Ebook Central. https://ebookcentral.proquest.com

Shumlich, E. J., & Fisher, W. A. (2018). Affirmative sexual consent? Direct and unambiguous consent is rarely included in discussions of recent sexual interactions. *The Canadian Journal of Human Sexuality, 27*(3), 248–260. https://doi.org/10.3138/cjhs.2017-0040

Shumlich, E. J., & Fisher, W. A. (2019). An information-motivation-behavioural skills model analysis of young adults' sexual behaviour patterns and regulatory requirements for sexual consent in Canada. *The Canadian Journal of Human Sexuality, 28*(3), 277–291. https://doi.org/10.3138/cjhs.2 018–0040

Shupe, S. (2022). *The influence of fraternity and sorority characteristics on alcohol exposure: Who is at risk?* (Electronic Theses and Dissertations). Paper 4061. https://dc.etsu.edu/etd/4061

Skrypnek, J. (2021, April 9). Explainer: What is rape culture and what does it look like in B.C.? *Langley Advance Times*. www.langleyadvancetimes.com/news/explainer-what-is-rape-culture-and-what-does-it-look-like-on-b-c/

Smith, M. (2018, July 23). Calgary police continue to examine sexual-assault cases as national unfounded rate drops. *Star Metro Calgary*. www.thestar.com/calgary/2018/07/23/calgary-police-continue-to-examine-sexual-assault-cases-as-national-unfounded-rate-drops.html

Solomon, A. H. (2018, August 10). Talking to college students about "the red zone". *Psychology Today*. www.psychologytoday.com/ca/blog/loving-bravely/201808/talking-college-students-about-the-red-zone

Sutha, J., Kailasapathy, P., & Jayakody, J. A. S. K. (2016). Integrated theoretical model for employees' intention to participate in non-mandatory trainings. *International Journal of Business and Management, 11*(11), 139–155. https://doi.org/10.5539/ijbm.v11n11p139

Thiessen, B., Williamson, L., & Buchanan, C. M. (2021). "Be proactive not reactive": Understanding gaps in student sexual consent education. *The Canadian Journal of Human Sexuality, 30*(3), 349–360. https://doi.org/10.3138/cjhs.2021-0003

Thomas, K. A., Sorenson, S. B., & Joshi, M. (2016). "Consent is good, joyous, sexy": A banner campaign to market consent to college students. *Journal of American College Health, 64*(8), 639–650. https://doi.org/10.1080/07448481.2016.1217869

Trusolino, M. (2017). "It's not about one bad apple": The 2007 York University Vanier residence rapes. In E. Quinlan, A. Quinlan, C. Fogel, & G. Taylor (Eds.), *Sexual violence at Canadian universities: Activism, institutional responses, and strategies for change* (pp. 79–92). ProQuest Ebook Central. https://ebookcentral.proquest.com

University of Alberta. (2016). Review of the University of Alberta's response to sexual assault. https://www.ualberta.ca/dean-of-students/media-library/documents/reports/uofasexualassaultreview.pdf

Vandervort, L. (2012). Affirmative sexual consent in Canadian law, jurisprudence, and legal theory. *Columbia Journal of Gender and Law, 23*(2), 395–442. https://ssrn.com/abstract=2132132

Vandiver, D. M., & Dupalo, J. R. (2013). Factors that affect college students' perceptions of rape: What is the role of gender and other situational factors?

International Journal of Offender Therapy and Comparative Criminology, 57(5), 592–592. https://doi.org/10.1177/0306624X12436797

VanTassel, B. (2020, January). *Culture and perspectives on a sexual assault policy.* https://www.msvu.ca/wp-content/uploads/2020/11/2020-CAPSAP-Report-1.pdf

Wasco, S. (2015). *Social norms marketing project: Project end evaluation report.* Pittsburgh Action Against Rape. https://doi.org/10.13140/RG.2.2.30108.51846

Weiss, K. G. (2010). Too ashamed to report: Deconstructing the shame of sexual victimization. *Feminist Criminology, 5*(3), 286–310. https://doi.org/10.1177/15570 85110376343

Willis, M., Hunt, M., Wodika, A., Rhodes, D. L., Goodman, J., & Jozkowski, K. N. (2019). Explicit verbal sexual consent communication: Effects of gender, relationship status, and type of sexual behavior. *International Journal of Sexual Health, 31*(1), 60–70. https://doi.org/10.1080/19317611.2019.1565793

Winiewski, W. (2017, December 8). Sexual assault reports on the rise in Saskatoon with possible link to #MeToo. *Global News.* https://globalnews.ca/news/3901183/sexual-assault-reports-saskatoon-metoo-global-movement/

Women's Legal Education & Action Fund (LEAF). (2020). *The law of consent in sexual assault.* www.leaf.ca/news/the-law-of-consent-in-sexual-assault/

Woodley, G. N., Jacques, C., Jaunzems, K., & Green, L. (2022, February 20). Mandatory consent education is a huge win for Australia – but consent is just one small part of navigating relationships. *The Conversation.* https://theconversation.com/mandatory-consent-education-is-a-huge-win-for-australia-but-consent-is-just-one-small-part-of-navigating-relationships-177456

Yule, K., & Grych, J. (2020). College students' perceptions of barriers to bystander intervention. *Journal of Interpersonal Violence, 35*(15–16), 2971–2992. https://doi.org/10.1177/0886260517706764

Zapp, D., Buelow, R., Soutiea, L., Berkowitz, A., & DeJong, W. (2021). Exploring the potential campus-level impact of online universal sexual assault prevention education. *Journal of Interpersonal Violence, 36*(5–6). https://journals.sagepub.com/doi/epub/10.1177/0886260518762449

4 Policies and programming

D. Scharie Tavcer

Introduction

Education to prevent SV has received considerable attention over the decades including an analysis of prevalence and prevention efforts. And growing in attention is consent education and prevention programming that extends beyond marketing campaigns and victim awareness. Criminology and sociology studies abound that confirm the problem of SV and illustrate myriad ways to address it. But we still have a way to go if we are to make a change. There are studies of about prevention education (DeKeseredy et al., 2018; Krebs et al., 2008; Richards, 2016), research about prevalence rates (Baum & Klaus, 2005; Fisher et al., 2000; Krebs et al., 2008; Muehlenhard et al., 2017; Paul & Gray, 2011; Smith et al., 2017), research about risk factors (Adams-Curtis & Forbes, 2004; Krebs et al., 2011; Lippy & DeGue, 2014; Marine, 2016), research about campus culture and PSI responses to the culture (e.g., fraternities, varsity athletics) (Cantalupo, 2011; Crosset, 2016; Janosik & Gregory, 2009; Koss & Cleveland, 1996), research about help-seeking behaviour and barriers (Nasta et al., 2005; Wolitzky-Taylor et al., 2011), research about BIPs (Banyard et al., 2007; Gidycz et al., 2011), and research about factors that contribute to the perpetration of SV (Adams-Curtis & Forbes, 2004; Lippy & DeGue, 2014; Marine, 2016).

A starting place is to look at policies and services at PSIs. Collins and Dunn (2018), in their work in the USA, argue that "despite institutional policy responses being framed as offering protection to victims, they are only enacted when threats are made to masculine privilege and when the institution needs to mitigate its own risk" (p. 374). We can extend this position to Canada and how PSI policies approach SV too. Through analyses of SV policies and procedures, and the surrounding literature, there remains a call for addressing the structural and systemic nature of SV – not just paperwork. When institutions prioritise increased policy protections on campuses, they nullify or dilute the ingrained racism and sexism in existing

DOI: 10.4324/9781003332671-4

laws, policies, procedures, historical, and contemporary institutional prac-tices (Bumiller, 2008; Hudson, 2006).

Magnussen and Shankar (2019) echo similar concerns in their critique of institutional SV policies. They acknowledge that an over-reliance on liabil-ity over-shadows the purpose of the policy that claims it serves all members of the campus community. Magnussen and Shankar (2019) and Krivoshey et al. (2013) offer that any stand-alone policy on SV should include the following:

(1) An extensive list of forms of SV, with descriptions to help people iden-tify their experiences.
(2) A clear map or outline of the reporting process, including contact infor-mation and possible consequences at each step.
(3) An emphasis that the complainant's identity will remain anonymous, including anonymous and third-party reporting options.
(4) A resource centre with staff that offers 24-hour accessibility to report-ing and providing support.

The literature is abundant about the keys to policy creation including that experts should be involved and that SV policies should be trauma-informed. Unfortunately, the analysis of policies at 130 PSIs reveals that changes are needed in this arena including offering students, faculty experts, and schol-ars the opportunity to contribute with policymakers.

Trauma-informed policies and services

Being trauma-informed means that the service provider, organisation, or the document and policy acknowledges that trauma informs how clients/students interact and that any policy should not retraumatise the client/stu-dent. Being trauma-informed means that an organisation seeks to (Center for Health Care Strategies, 2021):

• Realise the widespread impact of trauma and its paths for recovery.
• Recognise the signs and symptoms of trauma in clients, students, fami-lies, and staff.
• Integrate knowledge about trauma into policies, procedures, and practices.
• Actively avoid retraumatisation.

By contrast, taking a report of SV from a complainant for the purposes of determining the feasibility of an investigation requires a different type of interaction and engagement and one in which the institution is often the primary focus rather than the survivor. Discussions about the importance of having trauma-informed policy and services are a starting point for change, accountability, and supporting those who need them including bystanders and administrators (Browne, 2014; Iverson, 2017).

Policies at PSIs should be inclusive of the complexities and realities of sexual consent and refusal (Heenehan, 2019; Muehlenhard et al., 2017; Ostridge & O'Connor, 2020). Many efforts to prevent or respond to campus SV fail to be inclusive, leaving the structural dimensions of SV and its intersections with systems of oppression unaddressed (Colpitts, 2019). Sociocultural relevance indicates the need to customise programming to be accessible and attuned to the target audience's cultural attitudes and ideologies (Quam, 2017).

PSIs are reckoning with new challenges about how to prevent, combat, and address SV which should include questioning and unravelling a culture that has sustained patriarchal or colonial power dynamics that facilitate an unhealthy campus culture. Unfortunately, many PSIs are either unprepared or ill-equipped to dismantle those dynamics and systems. Or they take on a patriarchal protector role that allows them to isolate the perpetrator as an anomaly and that any survivors (read women) must be saved from the anomaly that is presumed to exist outside of the campus structure, not a part of it (Ahmed, 2018; Magnussen & Shankar, 2019). Or administrators lead the charge with revising policies rather than include subject expert faculty, researchers, and students (Shankar & Tavcer, 2021).

SV is a gendered issue (Cotter & Savage, 2019; Gretgrix & Farmer, 2022; Whittier, 2016; Worthen & Wallace, 2017), but the language used within policies tends to be un-gendered (Iverson, 2015). In Canada, 99% of sexual assaults against women are perpetrated by men, 87% of sexual assaults against both men and women are perpetrated by men (Benoit et al., 2015; Cotter & Savage, 2019).

Canadian data also show an increase in incidents of SV against trans individuals (Gunraj et al., 2014), Indigenous women and girls, women with disabilities, 2SLGBTQIA+ individuals, and women of colour (Gunraj et al., 2014; Mahony et al., 2017; Shankar, 2017); however, SV policies are not aligned with these realities, do not include policy language or protocols that acknowledge these realities, and often the people in charge of devising such policies have only a cursory understanding of the intersectional nature of SV (Gunraj et al., 2014; Iverson, 2017).

In the USA, one meta-analysis of 140 studies and interventions by DeGue et al. (2014) revealed that only three PSIs included content designed for specific racial/ethnic groups, and none specified sexual identity. Critical engagement with the role of gender in SV has remained nearly invisible in policy, marginalising trans, and gender diverse people. Policies must be used as not just a tool for response and support, but as "a mechanism to combat those power inequalities" (Abramsky et al., 2014, p. 2) and effect change to the campus culture that facilitates those inequalities.

The complaints process

A complaint is typically required to initiate an inquiry or investigation at a PSI. Often the term complaint is confused with reporting an incident to an authority external to the PSI. Plus, it is not always clear to whom a complaint should be made or that a report is a more official process that often removes the complainant's agency and involves outside justice authorities such as police. In Ahmed's (2021) book *Complaint!* her research underscored how inadequate and sometimes harmful, filing a complaint can be for students (or anyone impacted by SV), that what is supposed to happen does not always happen (e.g., ingrained support services, anonymity of complainants, clear communication), and that the process that unfolds can be quite different from a procedure even when procedures are followed. In her other work, Ahmed (2018, p. 17) states that "what might seem obvious (and the obvious is often obscured by being obvious – gender and racial inequality)" is one of several reasons that making a complaint is difficult to do but which makes it also necessary. And convoluted and legalese-laden policies aggravate matters as they lean towards protecting the PSI's image where the complainant is considered the damaging entity that is damaging the department, the student experience, or morale (p. 23).

A policy can be about what ought *not* to exist. Good practice requires practitioners to move beyond compliance (Iverson & Issadore, 2018; Jessup-Anger & Edwards, 2015), towards identifying and creating policies that can be part of a comprehensive sexual violence prevention and response programming for the entire campus community. How the issue is defined and constructed through policy language has implications for prevention and response, as well as culture shift. Although SV is gendered, cisgender heterosexual women are not the sole targets. SV policies unfortunately still describe it as affecting cisgender, heterosexual women, and they often fail to position the policy as something a male perpetrator does (Cahill, 2000). These gendered constructions sustain heteronormative and heterosexist constructions of SV and fail to identify other dimensions of identity as important (Wooten, 2015) and fail to acknowledge that prevention and intervention efforts need to be diverse, intersectional, and flexible.

The new normal in policymaking, according to Iverson and Issadore (2018), should be to edit and revise policies frequently in response to constantly changing guidelines, identities, and campus populations, culture, and demands. Existing policy work is too often in response to political will or liability reactions and lacks theoretical or empirical guidance or input from subject experts and those at the centre of the policy (DeGue et al., 2014; Levenson & D'Amora, 2007). Devising policy at PSIs tend to include administrators and lawyers rather than in-house staff and faculty experts, students, or external practitioners (Magnussen & Shankar, 2019; Shankar & Tavcer, 2021).

The structure of PSIs in Canada

Publicly funded PSIs are governed under a Ministry of Advanced Education. This Ministry is a government office run by elected officials from the governing provincial party at the time (e.g., the Liberal Party of Canada, The United Conservative Party, The New Democratic Party, Progressive Conservative Party, The Saskatchewan Party, the Bloc Québécois, and several others).[1]

Each Minister of Advanced Education (a.k.a. Ministry) puts their own spin on the types of leadership and direction for post-secondary education, which is dependent on which political party they are aligned with at the time. Political ideology, the financial market, the provincial budget, and deficit, as well as public pressure, all work to guide the work during the four years Ministers are in power. Some Ministries even direct labour market information and programmes at PSIs as well as register and regulate private or faith-based PSIs. Generally, most Ministries are responsible for:

- Approving programmes of study.
- Authorising universities to grant degrees.
- Funding public PSIs and other adult learning providers.
- Providing financial aid for learners & distributing provincial funds to PSIs.
- Registering and certifying apprentices.
- Supporting academic research and innovation.
- Planning and administering policies related to basic and applied research.
- Developing policy directions.

Legislating policies

Currently, not every Ministry of Advanced Education across Canada legislates that PSIs must have a stand-alone SV policy (e.g., a policy that is not embedded within another policy such as a Human Rights Policy), or education or prevention programming. Not every Ministry legislates its PSIs to have supports and services to address SV either. However, mandating policy directions for SV policy, education, and prevention programming, could address the gaps at PSIs across the provinces.

Despite a lack in legislation, and some provinces are stepping forward, but many appear ill-equipped to deal with SV (Magnussen & Shankar, 2019; Royster, 2017; Quinlan et al., 2016; Shen, 2017). For example, a 2014–2015 study at the University of Toronto (UofT) reported zero suspensions, expulsions, or disciplinary consequences despite the 137 informal complaints of sexual assault (Desai, 2016), but the UofT students who did formally report to campus authorities, were forced to sign confidentiality agreements ensuring that they did not discuss the incidents of SV (Desai, 2016; University of Toronto, 2022). Another example comes in 2016 from Brandon University which required complainants to sign a confidentiality agreement that included a statement that suspension or expulsion would be considered if they discussed their victimisation with anyone besides the PSI's counsellors (Laychuk, 2016). Clearly, such agreements are not trauma-informed but rather appear punitive towards complainants.

In another province, the University of Calgary (UofC) in 2018 reported it lacked grounds to expel a student because the assault had taken place prior to his enrolment at this Alberta PSI (Pike, 2018). The student pled guilty to sexual interference of a 13-year-old (through the CJS) and the university's decision resulted in public outrage that revealed gaps in the university's policy which did not address expulsion options if students are convicted of sexual offences. In fact, many PSIs choose *not* to exclude students with criminal records from enrolling in courses (Gravely, 2021), whereas some programmes still require students to be record free (e.g., in internships and practicum placements in social work, medicine, business, criminal justice programs) There is not a universal standard or provincial directive that requires PSIs address criminal convictions for SV specifically. Instead, often lacking is a clear policy language that itemises the consequences for non-academic misconduct such as being accused of, investigated for, or convicted of SV offences.

In the USA, according to Graham et al. (2017), 95% of American colleges and universities have policies that address campus SV. Policies can help shape social norms. The White House Task Force to Protect Students from Sexual Assault (the Task Force) was formed in response to the federal government's desire to prevent and address variations in SV policies across American campuses (Office of the Press Secretary, 2014). In 2014, the USA Task Force authored a Checklist[2] for Campus Sexual Misconduct Policies to provide PSIs with guidance and recommendations on how schools can make their policies more comprehensive.

The Checklist includes ten elements and suggests policy topics to be included in each element:

(1) An introduction.
(2) A detailed scope of the policy.
(3) Specific options for assistance.

(4) Identify the Title IX[3] Coordinator including their contact information.
(5) Definitions.
(6) Reporting policies and protocols.
(7) Investigation procedures and protocols.
(8) Grievance, adjudication, and appeal procedures.
(9) Prevention and education options.
(10) Training for employees.

Some Canadian Ministries have been as directive as the Taskforce, but there is no universality. Canadian Ministries of Advanced Education are just now stepping up to the plate to direct that their PSIs have stand-alone policies including SV education and prevention efforts. There are not only benefits to a universal directive but also disadvantages. An appropriate balance must be struck, ideally with input from subject experts, students, and external practitioners as well as acceptance of varied educational initiatives – PSIs should not think that one strategy, one type of programming, and/or one prevention initiative is all it will take to prevent or reduce SV. PSIs need to accept intersectionality and diversity in their policy, prevention, and services and ensure that they are trauma-informed and revisited frequently, and provide more than one option, method, and means to getting that education.

Environmental scans of PSIs

This project is one of several that are happening in Canada to address SV at PSIs. There are many passionate scholars and advocates who are working to help PSIs across Canada to do better. Not only to critique and collect data about policies and student experiences, but these projects also look to provide PSIs with recommendations to improve educational initiatives, for access to services, to include trauma-informed investigations and conduct processes, and to create responsive and intersectional policies, and more.

One national project is Courage to Act: Developing a Draft National Framework to Address and Prevent Gender-Based Violence at Post-Secondary Institutions in Canada (Khan et al., 2019). Courage to Act is a federally funded, multi-year national project led by Possibility Seeds and includes experts and advocates who are addressing all aspects of GBV and SV. Their environmental scan of GBV policies at PSIs (Tougas et al., 2021) is one source of data that were used in this project. Their scan used 15 key questions to review each province. Refer to Table 4.1 for their analysis.

Another national project is led by Dr. Shaheen Shariff, who along with iMPACTS[4] at McGill University, aim "to unearth, dismantle and prevent SV within universities, and ultimately in society, through evidence-based

Table 4.1 Courage to Act scan of Canadian legislation for PSIs.

Query	BC	MB	ON	PEI	QU	YK
Covers all publicly funded PSIs.	Yes	Yes	Yes	Yes	Yes	Yes
Requires PSIs to develop separate stand-alone SV policy for students.	Yes	Yes	Yes	No	Yes	No
Requires that SV policies include staff and/or that PSIs develop separate SV policies for staff.	No	No	No	No	No	No
Legislation includes the definition of SV or sexual misconduct.	Yes	Yes	Yes	Yes	Yes	Yes
Definition includes online behaviours/activities.	Yes	No	No	Yes	Yes	Yes
Policies must specifically include off-campus actions/ behaviours.	No	No	No	No	No	No
Policies must specify response protocols when a complaint or report is made.	Yes	Yes	Yes	Yes	Yes	Yes
Policies must specify timelines for reporting an incident to law enforcement.	No	No	No	No	Yes	No
Policies must include bystander intervention.	No	No	No	No	No	No
Policies must be in consultation with students.	Yes	Yes	Yes	Yes	Yes	No
Mandatory evaluation/review of policies.	Every 3 years	Every 5 years	Every 3 years	Every 3 years	Every 5 years	No
Evaluation/reviews of policy must be in consultation with students.	Yes	Yes	Yes	Yes	Yes	No
PSIs must release annual reports to public.	Yes	Yes	No	No	No	No
PSIs must provide annual reports to a governing body.	Yes	No	Yes	Yes	No	No
PSIs must provide annual reports to the Minister.	No	No	Yes	No	Yes	No
Minister may require PSIs to conduct surveys to determine effectiveness of policies.	Yes	No	Yes	No	No	No

Source: Adapted from Khan, Rowe, & Bidgood (2019).

research that will inform sustainable curriculum and policy change" (n.p.). Their multi-year project, funded by the Social Sciences and Humanities Research Council of Canada, is a collaboration with 24 PSIs that is wide in scope, and includes some international and American universities, but unfortunately it does not include a PSI from every Canadian province and territory or PSIs from provinces and territories with mandated legislation. Nevertheless, the results of this study will be immense and impactful and be another contribution towards helping PSIs do better.

Other projects are by the Council of Alberta University Students (2020) and Ending Violence Association of BC (2016) (Gray & Pin, 2017; Khan et al., 2019; Magnussen & Shankar, 2019). Their reviews highlight the gaps in how the country's PSIs address SV. In the USA, a review was conducted by Iverson (2015) which included an analysis of 22 university SV policies at American PSIs, finding that policies tend to "overemphasize risk, situating institutional agents as managers of the ubiquity of sexual violence on campus" (p. 60). Potter et al. (2000) in their examination of 100 American PSIs, also found that SV was conceptualised as risky for the institution, warranting risk reduction strategies. Additionally, their analysis revealed that policies rely on the deterrence model, the "fear of punishment by criminal law or university procedure" to prevent sexual violence perpetration (Potter et al., 2000, p. 1359).

These projects are important, but these efforts alone will not prevent or end SV or help PSIs change their culture to do better before, during, and after when complainants come forward. To achieve reductions in SV or an increase in reporting, policies, and diverse deliveries of programming must also be included in any prevention and education strategies. All things must be included to address SV from all directions. Iverson and Issadore (2018) argue for a "social – ecological model for understanding violence occurrence and recommends a systematic approach for prevention that considers all four levels of focus: individual, relationship, community, and society" (p. 60). PSIs should strive for policies and programming that clearly articulate that any incident of SV is not just an offence against the individual, but also an offence against the campus community (McGuire, 2004).

SV is a social justice issue, rooted in systems of power, privilege, and oppression that are differentially distributed among people of differing identities. Thus, policy authors must ensure the sociocultural relevance of SV policies for the multiplicity of identities represented on campuses, and "uncover power dynamics" embedded in policy (Phipps, 2010, p. 362). Such a structural analysis can reveal how privilege and advantage operate systemically, for example, that white victims and perpetrators receive benefits from their racial privilege; and how some dimensions of identity secure normative status (white, Christian, straight, able-bodied), while others are marginalised if not invisible (Iverson, 2017).

There's a dearth of research examining whether PSI SV policies impact the prevalence of campus SV and perhaps that should not be the sole aim of a policy. But to address this gap, DeJong et al. (2018) studied 24 universities participating in the 2015 Association of American Universities Campus Climate Survey on Sexual Assault and Sexual Misconduct. They linked 2014–2015 data from these universities' CSA policies and the prevalence findings from the 2015 Association of American Universities survey. Schools with policies that included information about their sexual assault response team had the lowest prevalence for both women and men, and schools that included topics describing grievance/adjudication procedures had lower CSA prevalence (Westat, 2015).

Aside from what's happening in the USA or in Canada, continued empirical analysis is needed to determine whether policies can be linked to a lower prevalence of CSA, but DeJong's et al. (2018) study provides an excellent starting point. Their study demonstrated that including certain topics within a policy can lower CSA. Five topics correlated with lower prevalence for both women and men and DeLong et al.'s study (2018) itemised the following: Describing the sexual assault response team, prohibiting the inclusion of a complainant's prior sexual conduct, stating that mediation is not an appropriate option, outlining the process for an appeal, and acknowledging that a hostile environment is not productive.

In short, all reports and reviews, studies, and scans reveal similar themes. Namely that PSIs have much work still to do to create campuses that are filled with consent and safety and where everyone is aware and trained. Paved with good intentions, some PSIs are leading the way towards a better campus culture, but with dwindling budgets and limited resources, what prevention, education, and response services are created, are limited in scope and depth. To truly change campus culture and the prevalence rates of SV, we must tackle the issue from all dimensions. Long-term and sustainable funding is needed that will support PSIs (for years) with the staff and experts, the programming and policies, and a variety of intervention and prevention services and supports.

The project's environmental scan of PSIs

This project scanned the publicly accessible websites of 130 English and French-speaking PSIs across Canada. The scan included their SV policies, any support services, and consent education programming. The project did not include an evaluation of any programming's efficacy.

This project collated surface-level information about what is currently happening at these PSIs regardless of whether they are legislated to provide SV prevention or have a stand-alone policy. In total, the environmental scan included 130 institutions inclusive of all provinces and territories. The scan queried the following:

(1) Does the PSI have a stand-alone sexual violence policy and procedures? If not, under what policy is it housed?
(2) Does the PSI have a sexual violence prevention office or an advocate staff person/expert who is dedicated to addressing sexual violence and supporting students and/or employees?
(3) What kinds of programming is available through the prevention office/ staff person? Is programming ad hoc or mandatory? Is it in person and/ or online? Is there specific consent-focused programming and if so, who gets that training?
(4) Does the PSI offer consent-focused education for employees, faculty, staff, and administrators? Or is it only directed at students and/or certain students?

Over 2020–2021, 96 out of 130 PSIs had a publicly available stand-alone SV policy and procedures document. The language in their policies focuses primarily on students but most are clear that all employees are also captured in their scope. What was consistent was that students are the focus front and centre of all out-facing PSI communications about SV. Most PSIs make information available and, in most cases, searching is easy on their websites. Services and programming are about and for students, which is important and makes sense. Students should be the primary focus. But supporting employees is crucial too if we are to shift campus culture, support everyone affected by SV, and establish fulsome structures in place to prevent, educate, and respond to SV.

Several provinces and one territory applied the mandated legislation requiring SV policy, education, and prevention programming. The absence of such legislation in one province prompted Magnussen and Shankar (2019) to examine how equipped PSIs really are to assist students in need. Their study examined whether Alberta's PSIs have an SV policy, is it easily accessible to students, and what is the ease with which students can access university resources and support services for SV. The results indicate that most institutions in Alberta simply do not have an accessible policy or support services for students in need.

Provinces and territories with legislation

British Columbia

Legislated in 2016, The *Sexual Violence and Misconduct Policy Act* mandated that all publicly funded PSIs in the province create stand-alone SV

Table 4.2 Scan of PSIs in British Columbia.

Number of PSIs scanned	18
Stand-alone sexual violence policy?	Yes
Legislated	Bill 23 The *Sexual Violence and Misconduct Policy Act* [SBC 2016] Chapter 23.
SV office or support person?	Yes, 14/18.
Is there consent-focused programming?	Yes, at 8/18.
Is consent-focused programming in person or online?	1 offers it online and in person and 7/18 offers it in person.
Is consent-focused programming ad hoc or mandatory?	Ad hoc.
Is all programming directed at students, staff, and faculty?	9/18 focuses on services for everyone while at the others it is unclear.

Source: Author

policies as well as prevention and education programming. The legislation requires that policies include several types of sexual misconduct, sexual misconduct prevention, and responses to that misconduct. And they must make their policies publicly available on their website.

Yukon

Before being legislated, in 2016, Yukon College created a stand-alone Sexualized Violence Prevention and Response Policy (2018). What is posted on their website is that in 2016, they offered staff at Yukon College (they became a university in 2020) training on how to respond to disclosures from a student or colleague. They also provided front-line staff across several departments including security officers similar training. The university also invites students and employees to visit endviolenceyukon.com or the Victoria Faulkner Women's Centre and Les EssentiELLES for information, resources, and support.

The university's counselling centre provides services for various issues such as anxiety and substance abuse, but it does not specifically identify support for prevention or interventions from SV (2018). And remains a gap and therefore no in person, online, or mandatory consent education programming is currently offered.

Manitoba

Manitoba passed Bill 3: *The Post-Secondary Sexual Violence and Sexual Harassment Policies Act* in 2016, which requires all post-secondary schools

Table 4.3 Scan of PSIs in the Yukon.

Number of PSIs scanned	1
Stand-alone sexual violence policy?	Yes.
Legislated	The *Yukon University Act* SY 2019, c. 15
SV office or support person?	No.
Is there consent-focused programming?	No.
Is consent-focused programming in person or online?	N/A
Is consent-focused programming ad hoc or mandatory?	N/A
Is all programming directed at students, staff, and faculty?	Yes

Source: Author

Table 4.4 Scan of PSIs in Manitoba.

Number of PSIs scanned	6
Stand-alone sexual violence policy?	Yes
Legislated	*Bill 3 The Post-Secondary Sexual Violence and Sexual Harassment Policies Act (Various Acts Amended)* and Bill 15: *The sexual violence awareness and prevention act (Advanced education administration act and private vocational institutions act amended).*
SV office or support person?	Yes, at 5/6.
Is there consent-focused programming?	Yes, at 4/7.
Is consent-focused programming in person or online?	3/7 offers programming both in person and online.
Is consent-focused programming ad hoc or mandatory?	Ad hoc. None make it mandatory.
Is all programming directed at students, staff, and faculty?	Yes.

Source: Author

in that province to have a sexual assault policy in place and for it to be developed with student input (Magnussen & Shankar, 2019).

Ontario

This province has legislation in place to dictate the responsibilities of PSIs across the province. Bill 132 – The *Sexual Violence and Harassment Action*

Table 4.5 Scan of PSIs in Ontario.

Number of PSIs scanned	33
Stand-alone sexual violence policy?	All but one (Redeemer University Christian College or their policy was not publicly available).
Legislated	*Bill 132, Sexual Violence and Harassment Action Plan Act (Supporting Survivors and Challenging Sexual Violence and Harassment), 2016.*
SV office or support person?	Yes, 31/33.
Is there consent-focused programming?	Yes, at 20/33.
Is consent-focused programming in person or online?	7/33 offers programming online and in person.
Is consent-focused programming ad hoc or mandatory?	1/33 makes it mandatory (UofT).
Is all programming directed at students, staff, and faculty?	22/33 offers programming for everyone with the others being no or unclear.

Source: Author

Plan Act (Supporting Survivors and Challenging Sexual Violence and Harassment), has been in place since March 2016. Of 33 PSIs reviewed in this study, all but one (Redeemer University College – a faith-based college) has a stand-alone SV prevention policy and procedures.

The Policy dictates that new requirements for SV policies at publicly assisted colleges and universities need to include wording that:

- A complainant acting in good faith who discloses or reports SV will not be subject to actions for violations of the institution's policies related to drug and alcohol use at the time the SV took place.
- During the institution's investigative process, students who share their experience of SV through disclosing, accessing support, and/or reporting to the university or college will not be asked irrelevant questions from the institution's staff or investigators, such as those relating to past sexual history or sexual expression.

Québec

The province of Québec has legislated SV prevention at all English and French colleges and universities across the province. The *Act to Prevent and Fight Sexual Violence in Higher Education Institution* (CQLR c P-22.1, July 2, 2021) states its purpose is,

Table 4.6 Scan of PSIs in Québec.

Number of PSIs scanned	21
Stand-alone sexual violence policy?	All but five don't have a policy or their policies were not publicly available.
Legislated	*Act to Prevent and Fight Sexual Violence in Higher Education Institutions* (2017, c. 32, c. I).
SV office or support person?	Yes, 7/21. The rest is unclear or not publicly searchable.
Is there consent-focused programming?	Yes at 6/17.
Is consent-focused programming in person or online?	The same 3/17 identify they have online as well as in person programming.
Is consent-focused programming ad hoc or mandatory?	3/17 makes it mandatory.
Is all programming directed at students, staff, and faculty?	9/17 offers programming for everyone with the others being no or unclear.

Source: Author

to strengthen actions to prevent and fight sexual violence in higher education institutions and to help foster a healthy and safe living environment for students and personnel members. To that end, the Act provides in particular for the implementation of prevention, awareness-raising, accountability, support and individual assistance measures.

Prince Edward Island

The *Post-Secondary Institutions Sexual Violence Policies Act* for Prince Edward Island (PEI) has been in place since 2018. Although the Act does not specify whether the policy must be separate and distinct from existing non-academic misconduct policies, it does dictate that all PSIs in the province must have stand-alone SV prevention policy and procedures.

Provinces and territories without legislation

Alberta

As of 2021, Alberta's Ministry for Advanced Education does not legislate its PSIs to have SV policy, prevention, or educational initiatives in place,

Table 4.7 Scan of PSIs in Prince Edward Island.

Number of PSIs scanned	3
Stand-alone sexual violence policy?	Yes
Legislated	Bill 41 *Prince Edward Island Post-Secondary Institutions Sexual Violence Policies Act* Chapter P-11.2, 2018 c.56.
SV office or support person?	Yes 2/3.
Is there consent-focused programming?	Yes at 3/3.
Is consent-focused programming in person or online?	3/3 in person.
Is consent-focused programming ad hoc or mandatory?	3/3 ad hoc.
Is all programming directed at students, staff, and faculty?	Yes.

Source: Author

but many colleges and universities are stepping up by creating policy and funding advocacy and support services.

An analysis of PSIs in Alberta by Magnussen and Shankar (2019) found 21 publicly funded institutions, five privately funded and five First Nations colleges, with 14 having designated stand-alone SV policies publicly available on their websites. Another six institutions had guidelines or protocols pertaining to SV as part of a larger policy on student conduct, discrimination, and harassment or students' rights and responsibilities. Two of the institutions were currently in the process of developing policies while the rest (nine out of 31) either did not have an SV policy or it was inaccessible. It is possible these nine institutions have policies in place, but they were not listed on their websites, which hinders students' and employees' ability to access and understand the information.

In September 2016, the Minister of Advanced Education called for all publicly funded PSIs to develop stand-alone SV policies that address training, prevention, complaint procedures, and response protocols (Derworiz, 2016), but did not mandate or legislate this directive. As of 2022, this project found that all but five publicly funded PSIs in Alberta had such a stand-alone policy.

Saskatchewan

There is no legislation dictating that PSIs in Saskatchewan address SV prevention. In the review of six PSIs, all but one has a stand-alone SV prevention

Table 4.8 Scan of PSIs in Alberta.

Number of PSIs scanned	26
Stand-alone sexual violence policy?	All but five either did not have a sexual violence policy or it was inaccessible.
Legislated	No.
SV office or support person?	Yes 16/26.
Is there consent-focused programming?	Yes at 7/26.
Is consent-focused programming in person or online?	6/26 offers it online or both.
Is consent-focused programming ad hoc or mandatory?	None make it mandatory.
Is all programming directed at students, staff, and faculty?	14/26 offers programming for everyone.

Source: Author

Table 4.9 Scan of PSIs in Saskatchewan.

Number of PSIs scanned	6
Stand-alone sexual violence policy?	All but one (Luther College which is affiliated with the University of Regina and presumably operates under the same policies).
Legislated	No.
SV office or support person?	Yes 3/3.
Is there consent-focused programming?	Yes at 3/6.
Is consent-focused programming in person or online?	2/6 offer it online or both.
Is consent-focused programming ad hoc or mandatory?	None make it mandatory.
Is all programming directed at students, staff, and faculty?	3/6 offers programming for everyone while at the others it is unknown.

Source: Author

policy and procedures. Luther College (a faith-based institution), which is a part of the University of Regina, does not have any policy that is publicly available through their web pages.

New Brunswick

As of 2021, New Brunswick does not have legislation that dictates PSIs must have policy and prevention initiatives, but they do encourage all PSIs to address the issue. In this review of eight PSIs, all but two have stand-alone SV prevention policy and procedures. Crandall University (a faith-based institution) and Kingswood University do not have any policy that is publicly available through their web pages.

Newfoundland and Labrador

As of 2021, there is no legislation dictating PSIs across Newfoundland and Labrador to address SV and prevention. Of the two PSIs we reviewed, the College of the North Atlantic does not have any policy that is publicly available through their web pages.

Northwest Territories

There is no legislation dictating PSIs in the Northwest Territories (NWT) address SV and prevention. There is only one publicly funded PSIs (Aurora College) in this territory and as of 2021, it does not have any SV policy that is publicly available through their web pages.

Table 4.10 Scan of PSIs in New Brunswick.

Number of PSIs scanned	8
Stand-alone sexual violence policy?	All but two (Crandall University and Kingswood University).
Legislated	No.
SV office or support person?	Yes 4/8.
Is there consent-focused programming?	Yes at 2/8.
Is consent-focused programming in person or online?	In person.
Is consent-focused programming ad hoc or mandatory?	Neither makes it mandatory.
Is all programming directed at students, staff, and faculty?	3/8 offers programming for everyone while at the others it is unknown.

Source: Author

Table 4.11 Scan of PSIs in Newfoundland and Labrador.

Number of PSIs scanned	2
Stand-alone sexual violence policy?	One does not (College of the North Atlantic).
Legislated	No.
SV office or support person?	Yes 1/2.
Is there consent-focused programming?	1 offers consent-focused programming.
Is consent-focused programming in person or online?	The one offers it in person.
Is consent-focused programming ad hoc or mandatory?	Neither make it mandatory.
Is all programming directed at students, staff, and faculty?	No.

Source: Author

Table 4.12 Scan of PSIs in the Northwest Territories.

Number of PSIs scanned	1
Stand-alone sexual violence policy?	No.
Legislated	No.
SV office or support person?	No.
Is there consent-focused programming?	No.
Is consent-focused programming in person or online?	N/A.
Is consent-focused programming ad hoc or mandatory?	N/A.
Is all programming directed at students, staff, and faculty?	N/A.

Source: Author

Nova Scotia

In 2017, the CFS put forth a list of recommendations on how the Nova Scotia government can best address SV on campuses. The first recommendation was to pass legislation that mandates sexual consent education for students, administration, faculty, and staff and that stand-alone sexual assault policies are reviewed every two years. A Memorandum of Understanding (2015) by the Council of Nova Scotia University Presidents involved 10 PSIs that committed to improve supports and SV prevention initiatives, but they are not governed by legislation to do so. In this analysis, most do have a stand-alone policy but only one has consent-focused programming.

Table 4.13 Scan of PSIs in Nova Scotia.

Number of PSIs scanned	8
Stand-alone sexual violence policy?	Yes.
Legislated	No.
SV office or support person?	Yes 6/8.
Is there consent-focused programming?	Yes at 7/8.
Is consent-focused programming in person or online?	Only 1 offers it online or both (Dalhousie).
Is consent-focused programming ad hoc or mandatory?	None make it mandatory.
Is all programming directed at students, staff, and faculty?	4/8 offers programming for everyone while at the others it is unknown.

Source: Author

Table 4.14 Scan of Nunavut PSIs.

Number of PSIs scanned	1
Stand-alone sexual violence policy?	Either does not have a sexual violence policy or it was inaccessible.
Legislated	No.
SV office or support person?	No.
Is there consent-focused programming?	No.
Is consent-focused programming in person or online?	N/A.
Is consent-focused programming ad hoc or mandatory?	N/A.
Is all programming directed at students, staff, and faculty?	No.

Source: Author

Nunavut

There is no legislation dictating PSIs in Nunavut address SV and prevention. There is only one publicly funded (Nunavut Arctic College) PSIs in this territory and as of 2021, it does not have any policy that is publicly available through their web pages.

The seven PSIs in focus

Seven institutions of varying sizes from several provinces were chosen from the 130 PSIs. Choice was precluded by accessibility for travel and funding support, ethics board approval, and SV advocates and staff at those institutions being receptive to participating.

A deeper look was important to examine how institutions address SV not just in policy and procedure documents, but from the staff and students who are a part of the campus community. Data collection included interviews and surveys with SV coordinators and advocates at these institutions as well as students. Initially, students were interviewed in person but when the COVID-19 pandemic closed universities in March 2020, the data collection method was revised to electronic surveys with recruitment via social media platforms and email. What follows is a presentation of information collected between 2019 and 2021 from seven institutions. Student interviews and findings will be presented in Chapter 5.

British Columbia

University of British Columbia Okanagan (UBCO) is a sister campus of the much larger University of British Columbia which is in Vancouver. The two institutions share policies and procedures for their student unions, research, student services, athletics, and more. UBCO acknowledges that their "campus and the city of Kelowna are located on the traditional, ancestral, and unceded territory of the Syilx Okanagan Nation" (UBCO, n.d.b.). As of 2020, more than 10,000 students from across Canada and 99 other countries are enrolled in undergraduate and graduate programmes at the UBCO campus. This campus was "purpose-built for the 21st century . . . in Kelowna in 2005" (UBCO, n.d.a.). Over 40% of undergraduate class sizes are capped at 30 students.

The British Columbia Ministry of Advanced Education and Skills Training legislated in 2016 of all PSIs in the province to have SV policy, procedures, and programming and UBCO does have a publicly accessible stand-alone SV policy and procedures.

There are several services provided through their residence advisors, counselling services, students union, and the Sexual Violence Prevention and Response Office (SVPRO). The SVPRO is a dedicated and physical space with staff to address SV on campus. This is not common at every PSI. The SVPRO (UBCO, n.d.c.),

> is a confidential place for those who have been impacted by any form of sexual or gender-based violence, harassment, or harm, regardless of where or when it took place. SVPRO aims to be a safer space for all UBC students, faculty, and staff by respecting each person's unique and multiple identities and experiences. All genders and sexualities are welcome. We do not believe sexualized violence is an inevitability. SVPRO works to educate the UBC community in the prevention of sexual and

gender-based violence from an intersectional, decolonizing, anti-oppression framework.

The SVPRO at UBCO offers many types of support and guidance for students including reporting options, medical options and information, information for faculty and staff, on- and off-campus resources, educational information, workshops, policy information, and invitations to volunteer and get involved. They offer support such as safety planning, supporting academic accommodations, reporting options, counselling referrals, and more. It appears that most services are targeted for students only. Their services are after the fact with only some prevention and education initiatives such as defining SV.

There does not appear to be an educational programme that specifically addresses consent. The SVPRO does offer various workshops, which appear to be in person only or on a request or an ad hoc basis.

Alberta

MacEwan University

For the 2020–2021 academic year, MacEwan University had approximately 12,000 full-time and part-time students in credit programmes and over 18,000 full-time and part-time students (MacEwan University, n.d.a.). The average age of students is 24 years, with over 60% being female. MacEwan acknowledges that

> the land on which we gather in Treaty Six Territory is the traditional gathering place for many Indigenous people. We honour and respect the history, languages, ceremonies and culture of the First Nations, Métis and Inuit who call this territory home. kihêw waciston, which means 'eagle's nest' in Cree, is a home away from home for MacEwan University's Indigenous students.

The Alberta Ministry of Advanced Education does not legislate PSIs to have SV policy, procedures, and programming, but MacEwan has publicly accessible and stand-alone SV policy and procedures and programming. They also provide several support services through their residence advisors, counselling services, students union, and the Office of Sexual Violence Prevention, Education, and Response (MacEwan University, n.d.b.). The Office acknowledges that "we all play a part in creating a safe and supportive campus." The Office, [is] "committed to creating a culture of consent and ending sexual violence" as well as providing support, interpreting policy, and "creating positive change."

In 2022, MacEwan adopted the *It Takes All of Us* online consent education module created at Concordia University. To date, it is not mandatory and only directed at students. In 2019, MacEwan University surveyed students and employees to learn about their perspectives and experiences with SV on and off campus. The MacEwan University Sexual Violence Climate Survey (2020) revealed that

- 49% of students and 56% of employees reported that, in their lifetime, someone had sexual contact with them that they did not consent to.
- 12% of students and 3% of employees reported that, in the previous year, someone had sexual contact with them that did not consent to.
- 38% of students and 19% of employees reported that, in the previous year, someone had made sexual comments, advances, gestures, or jokes that were unwelcome.
- 16% of students and 6% of employees indicated that, in the previous year, someone had shown them sexual pictures, photos or videos that they did not want to see.

Mount Royal University

For the 2019–2020 academic year, Mount Royal University (MRU) had over 14,000 students of which 1.9% were international students and 6.1% students identified as Indigenous (Mount Royal University, n.d.). MRU acknowledges it is

> located in the traditional territories of the Niitsitapi (Blackfoot) and the people of the Treaty 7 region in Southern Alberta, which includes the Siksika, the Piikani, the Kainai, the Tsuut'ina, and the Hare Nakoda. The City of Calgary is also home to the Métis Nation. Region 3

The Alberta Ministry of Advanced Education does not legislate PSIs to have SV policy, procedures, and programming, but MRU has a stand-alone policy and procedures and programming. In 2022, a working group is revising the 2017 policy.

MRU provides several support services through their residence advisors, counselling and wellness, and the Dating, Domestic, and Sexual Violence Education and Response Specialist. As of 2022, MRU does not have a physical space for a SV response centre but there is the Specialist and an Office of Safe Disclosure which "provides a range of services related to equity, human rights, discrimination, and other safe disclosure concerns. Students, staff, faculty, and all other members of the Mount Royal community are all welcome to access these services" (Mount Royal University, 2022b).

The Dating, Domestic, and Sexual Violence Education and Response Specialist is one SV advocate staff person who resides under the Wellness Services department. As part of her work, she leads the Dating, Domestic, and Sexual Violence Committee (DDSVC) with the goal to provide "a safe and supportive environment to learn, live, and work by providing specialized support and education" (Mount Royal University, 2022a). The Specialist offers support and guidance to those wishing to report an incident of SV and to also advocate for academic accommodations, provide safety planning, referrals, and resource services on and off campus. The Specialist shares the policy and procedures, reporting options, and how to get support or give support to those who disclose. Educational programming includes in-person seminars on an ad hoc basis with some scheduled regularly throughout the academic year such as Building the Love you Want Miniseries, Survivor Love Letter Button Making, the I Believe You Campaign, Managing Breakups Discussion Series, The Kind Men Campaign, and the Stepping Up Dating Violence Prevention training program.

MRU has the Stepping Up program which "is a relationship violence prevention program open to all students . . . [and brings] together students of all backgrounds, ages and genders" (Mount Royal University, 2022c). Interactive activities help participants identify the differences between healthy, unhealthy, and abusive behaviours, and where to turn if they or someone they know needs help. The two key components are peer-facilitated workshop sessions and participant community projects following the workshop sessions. Any consent-based education is incorporated into some of the earlier workshops as well as information on the Relationship Violence Prevention & Research Centre website (which is led by the Department of Child Studies and Social Work).

Manitoba

As of 2020, the University of Winnipeg (UW) had a total of 9,691 students (9,396 undergraduate students and 295 graduate students). Almost 10% of the student population self-identifies as Indigenous and over 14.3% are international students (UW, n.d.a.). The UW acknowledges that they are "gathered on ancestral lands, on Treaty One Territory. These lands are the heartland of the Métis people. We acknowledge that our water is sourced from Shoal Lake 40 First Nation" (UW, n.d.b.).

The Manitoba Ministry of Advanced Education, Skills, and Immigration legislates that PSIs have SV policy, procedures, and programming. UW has a publicly accessible stand-alone SV policy and procedures and programming. There are several services provided through their residence advisors, counselling services, students union, and the Human Rights and Diversity

Office (HRDO). SV programming is housed under the HRDO including a Sexual Violence Response Team which is "a small group of senior staff who coordinate accommodations and resources for students who have experienced sexual violence" (University of Winnipeg, n.d.d.).

The response team includes Human Rights and Sexual Violence Advisors who can be reached via phone, text, or email. Students can also report an incident online through the REES software system.[5] They also offer students options, resources, support, academic accommodations, or referrals to external agencies. Their educational programming includes information about SV and myths, rape culture, intersectionality, and website information about consent. From what appears on their website, they offer no specific consent education course offered online or in person to students or employees.

Ontario

For 2020, the University of Ottawa had over 37,000 undergraduate students (21,904 females) and 7,244 graduate students (4,055 females) and enrols international students from over 150 countries. The University (n.d.b.) pays

> respect to the Algonquin people, who are the traditional guardians of this land. We acknowledge their long-standing relationship with this territory, which remains unceded. We pay respect to all Indigenous people in this region, from all nations across Canada, who call Ottawa home. We acknowledge the traditional knowledge keepers, both young and old. And we honour their courageous leaders: past, present, and future.

The Ontario Ministry of Colleges and Universities legislates all PSIs to have SV policy, procedures, and programming. The University of Ottawa (UO) has a publicly accessible stand-alone SV policy and procedures, and several services are provided through their residence advisors, counselling services, students union, and the Human Rights Office.

The UO has a SV support and prevention services through a group of staff who reside under the Human Rights Office. They offer information and support for anyone who has experienced or witnessed SV, including reporting options (with details about confidentiality and what to expect after submitting a report), how to support a friend, on-campus and off-campus resources, education, and information, becoming a volunteer, events, policies, and training opportunities. UO has several webpages offering educational and prevention documents such as quick facts, the effects of SV, drugs, and alcohol, cyber-sexual violence, and consent education, and online disclosure (UO, n.d.a.).

The consent education is limited to out-facing information and links only, but the office offers two training modules (What to do When Someone Discloses an Alleged Incident of Sexual Violence and Mobilizing the Bystanders) (UO, n.d.c.). Both are in person and provided at the request of students or employees.

Québec

For the 2020–2021 academic year, Concordia University had approximately 37,000 undergraduate students, 9,500 graduate students, and approximately 9,900 international students (Concordia University, n.d.b.). And close to 45% of their 200-, 300-, and 400-level courses have fewer than 60 students. Their undergraduate and graduate programmes combined have almost an even split of female students 23,556 (19,367 undergraduate) and male students 23,225 (17,905 undergraduate). Concordia University acknowledges that it is located on unceded Indigenous lands. "The Kanien'kehá:ka Nation is recognized as the custodians of Tiohtià:ke/Montréal."

The Québec Ministry of Higher Education legislates all PSIs to have SV policy, procedures, and programming. Concordia has a publicly accessible stand-alone SV policy and procedures, and several services are provided through their residence advisors, counselling services, students union, and the Sexual Assault Resource Centre (SARC) Concordia University (n.d.a.).

SARC offers a physical and virtual space for students and employees who have been affected by SV; services to students, staff, and faculty who have immediate concerns about SV require information or support, counselling, or training. SARC values a "survivor-centred, feminist, and intersectional" approach. SARC offers crisis response, trauma-informed counselling, referrals to on-campus or off-campus resources, or peer support groups, as well as in person or online training and workshops by request. Their website provides information about the policy and procedures, myths, and statistics (about consent, SV, harassment, and misconduct), and supports for academic accommodations. SARC provides (Concordia University, n.d.c.),

> confidential and non-judgmental support and services to Concordia University students, staff and faculty who have been affected by sexual violence. Through education and raising awareness we are committed to preventing sexual violence on campus and beyond.

Concordia University (and other PSIs in Québec) has mandatory online (or in person) SV prevention and consent education training for students and employees. The introductory module, *It Takes All of Us*, "is preventive in nature and explores the basics of sexual violence . . . along with information and tools regarding consent, bystander intervention, and supporting survivors." It was created by experts at Concordia and is generously shared with any PSI in Canada to adapt to their campus community.

Concordia is the only PSI that mandates consent education training. The training must be completed by October of the upcoming academic year. It is mandatory for employees and students and can be accomplished through their e-learning portal or in person. Concordia's mandatory "sexual violence awareness and prevention training is fundamental in creating a safe and supportive working and learning environment at Concordia and is a legal requirement as outlined by Bill 151." Additionally, faculty and staff are required to complete annual training for SV awareness and prevention where new content is released "each year at the beginning of May and a generous timeline for completion will be given. Specific dates for completion will be communicated each year."

Their second module, *Systems of Oppression and Intersectionality Training Module*, (Concordia University, n.d.d.) is not mandatory, and offers a "way to learn about the role of power dynamics as a root of sexual violence."

New Brunswick

As of 2021, St. Thomas University (STU) has just over 1,800 undergraduate students with class sizes capped at 60. STU is a part of the University of New Brunswick's Fredericton campus, and the two institutions share facilities for their student unions, libraries, athletics, etc. St. Thomas University acknowledges that "the land on which we gather is the traditional territory of the Wolastoqiyik, Wəlastəkewiyik/Maliseet whose ancestors along with the Mi'Kmaq/Mi'kmaw and Passamaquoddy/Peskotomuhkati Tribes/ Nations signed Peace and Friendship Treaties with the British Crown in the 1700s" (STU, n.d.b.).

The New Brunswick Ministry for Post-Secondary Education, Training and Labour does not legislate PSIs to have SV policy, procedures, and programming. STU has a publicly accessible stand-alone SV policy and procedures, and several services are provided through their residence advisors, counselling services, students union, and the Campus Sexual Assault Support and Advocacy (CSASA).

There are two Sexual Violence Support Advocates at CSASA who support survivors of SV as well provide services. Their physical space allows them to provide services for "enhancing the response and prevention of sexual violence in our communities . . . [and] a safe place to feel heard, believed, and validated while they work to explore options available to survivors" (STU, n.d.c.). CSASA has an optional and online bystander training program aimed at addressing the issues of SV. The *Seeds of Change: Bystander Skills that Transform Cultures of Sexual Violence*, is for students (STU, n.d.a.). The workshop seeks "to empower communities to make change in their own lives, perpetuating a culture of violence intolerance" (New Brunswick Canada, 2019).

Conclusion

This chapter presented the findings from the environmental scan from the research project. It provided a Canada-wide overview of what policies and programming exist and narrowed to focus on provinces and territories with SV legislation and then focused on results from the even PSIs. While nearly all PSIs in Canada have stand-alone SV policies, very few have consent-focused programming or support and intervention services. And even fewer have online or mandatory consent education training or programming.

Notes

1 The Yukon territory is split between the Yukon Liberals and the Yukon Party, which is what the Yukon Progressive Conservative Party renamed itself in 1992. Canada's two far-northern territories, the Northwest Territories and Nunavut, have very small parliaments that don't use political parties: https://thecanadaguide.com/government/political-parties/.
2 Checklist elements and topics can be found www.justice.gov/archives/ovw/page/file/910271/download
3 To learn more about Title IX visit https://www2.ed.gov/about/offices/list/ocr/docs/tix_dis.html
4 www.mcgill.ca/definetheline/impacts
5 REES (Respect, Educate, Empower Survivors) is an online reporting for sexual violence on campus.

References

Abramsky, T., Devries, K., Kiss, L., Nakuti, J., Kyegombe, N., Starmann, E., & Watts, C. (2014). Findings from the SASA study: A cluster randomized controlled trial to assess the impact of a community mobilization intervention to prevent violence against women and reduce HIV risk in Kampala, Uganda. *BMC Medicine*, *12*(1), 1–17. https://doi.org/10.1186/s12916-014-0122-5
Adams-Curtis, L. E., & Forbes, G. B. (2004). College women's experiences of sexual coercion: A review of cultural, perpetrator, victim, and situational variables. *Trauma, Violence & Abuse*, *5*(2), 91–122. https://doi.org/10.1177/1524838003262331

Ahmed, S. (2018). Complaint as feminist pedagogy. In K. Chandrashekar, K. Lacroix, & S. Siddiqui (Eds.), *Annual review of critical psychology* (Vol. 15). ISSN: 1746–739X Special Issue *Sex and Power in the University*. https://feministkilljoys.com/2021/06/16/complaint-as-feminist-pedagogy/

Ahmed, S. (2021). *Complaint!* Duke University Press.

Association of American Universities. (2015). *Climate survey on sexual assault and sexual misconduct*. www.aau.edu/issues/climate-survey-sexual-assault-and-sexual-misconduct

Banyard, V. L., Moynihan, M. M., & Plante, E. G. (2007). Sexual violence prevention through bystander education: An experiment evaluation. *Journal of Community Psychology, 35*(4), 463–481. https://doi.org/10.1002/jcop.20159

Baum, K., & Klaus, P. (2005). *Violence victimization of college students, 1995–2002*. National Crime Victimization Survey. www.ocpaoh.org/Campus%20Safety/Violent%20Victimization%20of%20College%20Students.pdf

Benoit, C., Shumka, L., Phillips, R., Kennedy, M. C., & Belle-Isla, L. (2015). Issue brief: Sexual violence against women in Canada. *The Federal-Provincial-Territorial Senior Officials for the Status of Women*. https://cfc-swc.gc.ca/svawc-vcsfc/issue-brief-en.pdf

Bill 3: The Post-Secondary Sexual Violence and Sexual Harassment Policies Act (Various Acts Amended).

Bill 15: *Manitoba the sexual violence awareness and prevention act (Advanced education administration act and private vocational institutions act amended)*. SM 2016, c.20. 1st session, 41st Legislature. (Assented to 2016). https://web2.gov.mb.ca/bills/41-1/b015e.php#Explanatory%20Note

Bill 23: *British Columbia sexual violence and misconduct policy act*. SBC 2016, c.23.(Assented19May2016).www.bclaws.gov.bc.ca/civix/document/id/complete/statreg/16023_01

Bill 41: *Prince Edward island post-secondary institutions sexual violence policies act*. SPEI, c. 56. (Assented to 2018). www.princeedwardisland.ca/sites/default/files/legislation/p-11-2-post-secondary_institutions_sexual_violence_policies_act.pdf

Bill 132: *Ontario sexual violence and harassment action plan act (Supporting survivors and challenging sexual violence and harassment)*. SO 2016, c.2. (Assented 8 March 2016). www.ola.org/sites/default/files/node-files/bill/document/pdf/2016/2016-03/bill – text-41–1-en-b132ra.pdf

Bill 151: *Québec an act to prevent and fight sexual violence in higher education institutions*. SQ 2017, c. 32 c. 1. (Assented to 2017). www.legisquebec.gouv.qc.ca/en/pdf/cs/P-22.1.pdf

Browne, R. (2014, October 30). Why don't Canadian universities want to talk about sexual assault? *Maclean's*. www.macleans.ca/education/unirankings/why-dont-canadian-universities-want-to-talk-about-sexual-assault/

Bumiller, K. (2008). *In an abusive state: How neoliberalism appropriated the feminist movement against sexual violence*. Duke University Press.

Cahill, A. J. (2000). Foucault, rape, and the construction of the feminine body. *Hypatia, 15*(1), 43–63. https://doi.org/10.1111/j.1527-2001.2000.tb01079.x

Cantalupo, N. (2011). Burying our heads in the sand: Lack of knowledge, knowledge avoidance and the persistent problem of campus peer sexual violence. *Loyola University Chicago Law Journal, 43*, 205. https://scholarship.law.georgetown.edu/facpub/634

Center for Health Care Strategies. (2021). *What is trauma-informed care?* www.traumainformedcare.chcs.org/what-is-trauma-informed-care/

Collins, V. E., & Dunn, M. (2018). The invisible/visible claims to justice: Sexual violence and the university camp(us). *Contemporary Justice Review, 21*(4), 371–395. https://doi.org/10.1080/10282580.2018.1531717

Colpitts, E. M. (2019). *An intersectional analysis of sexual violence policies, responses, and prevention efforts at Ontario universities* (Dissertation). https://yorkspace.library.yorku.ca/xmlui/bitstream/handle/10315/36778/Colpitts_Emily_M_2019_PhD.pdf?sequence=2&isAllowed=y

Concordia University. (n.d.a). *About SARC.* www.concordia.ca/conduct/sexual-assault/about.html

Concordia University. (n.d.b). *Fast facts.* www.concordia.ca/about/fast-facts.html

Concordia University. (n.d.c). *Sexual violence training.* www.concordia.ca/conduct/sexual-violence/training.html

Concordia University. (n.d.d). *Systems of oppression and intersectionality training.* www.concordia.ca/conduct/sexual-violence/the-systems-of-oppression-and-intersectionality-training-module-is-now-available-to-concordia-students.html

Cotter, A., & Savage, L. (2019). *Gender-based violence and unwanted sexual behaviour in Canada, 2018: Initial findings from the Survey of Safety in Public and Private Spaces.* https://www150.statcan.gc.ca/n1/pub/85-002-x/2019001/article/00017-eng.htm

Council of Nova Scotia University Presidents. (2015). *Changing the culture of acceptance: Recommendations to address sexual violence on university campuses.* https://novascotia.ca/lae/pubs/docs/changing-the-culture-of-acceptance.pdf

Council of Alberta University Students. (2020). CAUS releases campus sexual violence white paper. www.caus.net/news/2020/2/10/caus-releases-campus-sexualviolence-white-paper

Crosset, T. W. (2016). Athletes, sexual assault, and universities' failure to address rape-prone subcultures on campus. In S. C. Wooten & R. W. Mitchell (Eds.), *The crisis of campus sexual violence: Critical perspectives on prevention and response* (pp. 74–92). Routledge. https://psycnet.apa.org/record/2016-02132-005

DeGue, S., Valle, L. A., Holt, M. K., Massetti, G. M., Matjasko, J. L., & Tharp, A. T. (2014). A systematic review of primary prevention strategies for sexual violence perpetration. *Aggression and Violent Behavior, 19*(4), 346–362. https://doi.org/10.1016/j.avb.2014.05.004

DeKeseredy, W. S., Hall-Sanchez, A., & Nolan, J. (2018). College campus sexual assault: The contribution of peers' proabuse informational support and attachments to abusive peers. *Violence against Women, 24*(8), 922–935. https://doi.org/10.1177/1077801217724920

DeLong, S. M., Graham, L. M., Magee, E. P., Treves-Kagan, S., Gray, C. L., McClay, A. M., Zarnick, S. M., Kupper, L. L., Macy, R. J., Ashley, O. S., Pettifor, A., Moracco, K. E., & Martin, S. L. (2018). Starting the conversation: Are campus sexual assault policies related to the prevalence of campus sexual assault? *Journal of Interpersonal Violence*, *33*(21), 3315–3343. https://doi.org/10.1177/0886260518798352

Derworiz, C. (2016, September 8). Province expects all publicly funded Alberta universities and colleges to adopt sexual assault policies. *Calgary Herald.* https://calgaryherald.com/news/local-news/campus-safety

Desai, S. (2016, August 9). How Canadian universities are failing sexual assault survivors. *Now Toronto.* https://nowtoronto.com/news/how-canadianuniversities-are-failing-sexual-assault-survivors/

Ending Violence Association of BC. (2016). *Campus Sexual Violence: Guidelines for a Comprehensive Response.* https://endingviolence.org/wp-content/uploads/2016/05/EVABC_CampusSexualViolenceGuidelines_vF.pdf

Fisher, B. S., Cullen, E. T., & Turner, M. G. (2000). *The sexual victimization of college women* (NCJ 182369). US Department of Justice. www.ojp.gov/pdffiles1/nij/182369.pdf

Gidycz, C. A., Orchowski, L. M., & Berkowitz, A. D. (2011). *Preventing sexual aggression among college men: An evaluation of a social norms and bystander intervention program.* https://doi.org/10.1177/1077801211409727

Graham, L. M., Treves-Kagan, S., Magee, E. P., DeLong, S. M., Ashley, O. S., Macy, R. J., . . . Bowling, J. M. (2017). Sexual assault policies and consent definitions: A nationally representative investigation of United States colleges and universities. *Journal of School Violence*, *16*, 243–258. https://doi.org/10.1080/15388220.2017.1318572

Gravely, A. (2021, September 7). *A natural progression.* www.insidehighered.com/admissions/article/2021/09/07/congress-looks-remove-criminal-history-questions-admissions

Gretgrix, E., & Farmer, C. (2022). Heteronormative assumptions and expectations of sexual violence: Language and inclusivity within sexual violence policy in Australian Universities. *Sex Res Soc Policy.* https://doi.org/10.1007/s13178-022-00718-7

Gunraj, A., Wandio, C., Abdullah, S., Komiotis, W., Marshall, P., Mustachi, J., Rahim, C., & Witelson, T. (2014). Sexual assault policies on campus: A discussion paper. *METRAC Action on Violence.* www.metrac.org/wp-content/uploads/2014/11/final.formatted.campus.discussion.paper_.26sept14.pdf

Heenehan, F. M. (2019). Best practices in consent education: An analysis. *The Vermont Connection*, *40*(16), 115–122. https://scholarworks.uvm.edu/tvc/vol40/iss1/16

Hudson, B. (2006). Beyond white man's justice: Race, gender and justice in late modernity. *Theoretical Criminology*, *10*(1), 29–47. https://doi.org/10.1177/1362480606059981

Iverson, S. V. (2015). A policy discourse analysis of sexual assault policies in higher education. In S. C. Wooten & R. W Mitchell (Eds.), *The crisis of campus sexual violence: Critical perspectives on prevention and response* (pp. 15–32). Routledge/Taylor & Francis Group. www.taylorfrancis.com/chapters/edit/10.4324/9781315725604-2/policy-discourse-analysis-sexual-assault-policies-higher-education-susan-iverson

Iverson, S. V. (2017). Mapping identities: An intersectional analysis of sexual violence policies. In J. Harris & C. Linder (Eds.), *Intersections of identity and sexual violence on campus: Centering minoritized students' experiences* (pp. 214–232).

Stylus. https://styluspub.presswarehouse.com/browse/book/9781620363881/ Intersections-of-Identity-and-Sexual-Violence-on-Campus

Iverson, S. V., & Issadore, M. N. (2018). Going upstream: Policy as sexual violence prevention and response. *New Directions for Student Services, 161,* 59–69. https://doi.org/10.1002/ss.20253

Janosik, S. M., & Gregory, D. E. (2009). *The Clery Act,* campus safety, and the perceptions of senior student affairs officers. *NASPA Journal, 46*(2), 338–357. https://doi.org/10.2202/1949-6605.6039

Jessup-Anger, J., & Edwards, K. E. (Eds.). (2015). Beyond compliance: Addressing sexual violence in higher education. In L. K. Badke (Ed.) (2016), *Beyond compliance: A multi-case study analysis of university behavior and policy negotiation in response to the dear colleague letter on campus sexual violence* (Order No. 10391462). Available from ProQuest Dissertations & Theses Global. (1874468217). http://libproxy.mtroyal.ca/login?url=www.proquest.com/dissertations-theses/ beyond-compliance-multi-case-study-analysis/docview/1874468217/se-2

Khan, F., Rowe, C. J., & Bidgood, R. (2019). *Courage to act: Developing a national draft framework to address and prevent gender-based violence at post-secondary institutions in Canada.* https://static1.squarespace.com/static/5d482d9fd8b74f0001c02192/ t/5ff87e2cd88d0c4f5730cca1/1610120778285/EN_Courage+to+Act+Report.pdf

Koss, M. P., & Cleveland, H. H. (1996). Athletic participation, fraternity membership, and date rape: The question remains – Self-selection or different causal processes? *Violence Against Women, 2*(2), 180–190. https://doi.org/10.1177/1077 801296002002005

Krebs, C. P., Lindquist, C. H., & Barrick, K. (2011). The historically black college and university campus sexual assault (HBCU-CSA) study. *The National Institute of Justice.* www.ojp.gov/pdffiles1/nij/grants/233614.pdf

Krebs, C. P., Lindquist, C. H., Warner, T. D., Fisher, B. S., & Martin, S. L. (2008). The campus sexual assault (CSA) study. *US Department of Justice.* www.ojp.gov/ pdffiles1/nij/grants/221153.pdf

Krivoshey, M. S., Adkins, R., Hayes, R., Nemeth, J. M., & Klein, E. G. (2013). Sexual assault reporting procedures at Ohio colleges. *Journal of American College Health, 61*(3), 142–147. https//doi.org/10.1080/07448481.2013.769260

Laychuk, R. (2016, April 5). Brandon University sexual assault victims forced to sign contract that keeps them silent. *CBC News.* www.cbc.ca/news/canada/ manitoba/brandon-university-behavioural-contract-1.3520568

Levenson, J. S., & D'Amora, D. A. (2007). Social policies designed to prevent sexual violence: The emperor's new clothes? *Criminal Justice Policy Review, 18*(2), 168–199. https://doi.org/10.1177/0887403406295309

Lippy, C., & DeGue, S. (2014). Exploring alcohol policy approaches to prevent sexual violence perpetration. *Trauma, Violence & Abuse, 17*(1), 26–42. https:// doi.org/10.1177/1524838014557291

MacEwan University. (n.d.a). *Facts and figures.* www.macewan.ca/wcm/discover/ ourstory/factsandfigures/index.htm

MacEwan University. (n.d.b). *The office of sexual violence prevention, education and response.* www.macewan.ca/campus-life/office-of-sexual-violence-prevention-education-and-response/

MacEwan University. (2020). *MacEwan University sexual violence climate survey.* www.macewan.ca/c/documents/osvper_climate_survey_2020.pdf

Magnussen, J., & Shankar, I. (2019). Where is it? Examining post-secondary students' accessibility to policies and resources on sexual violence. *The Canadian Journal of Higher Education, 49*(2), 90–108. https://doi.org/10.47678/cjhe.v49i2.188203

Mahony, T. H., Jacob, J., & Hobson, H. (2017). *Women and criminal justice system* [Catalogue no, 89–503-X]. https://www150.statcan.gc.ca/n1/pub/89-503-x/2015001/article/14785-eng.pdf

Marine, S. (2016). Combating sexual violence in the ivy league: Reflections on politics, pain, and progress. In S. C. Wooten & R. W. Mitchell (Eds.), *The crisis of campus sexual violence: Critical perspectives on prevention and response* (pp. 55–73). Routledge. www.taylorfrancis.com/chapters/edit/10.4324/9781315725604-4/combating-sexual-violence-ivy-league-susan-marine

McGuire, D. L. (2004). "It was like all of us had been raped": Sexual violence, community mobilization, and the African American freedom struggle. *The Journal of American History, 91*(3), 906–931. https://doi.org/10.2307/3662860

Mount Royal University. (2022a). *Dating, domestic, sexual violence.* www.mtroyal.ca/CampusServices/WellnessServices/dating-domestic-sexual-violence.htm

Mount Royal University. (2022b). *The office of safe disclosure.* www.mtroyal.ca/OfficeOfSafeDisclosure/index.htm

Mount Royal University. (2022c). *Relationship violence prevention & research centre.* www.mtroyal.ca/ProgramsCourses/FacultiesSchoolsCentres/HealthCommunityEducation/Departments/ChildStudiesandSocialWork/RelationshipViolencePrevention/GetInvolved/SteppingUp/index.htm

Mount Royal University. (n.d.). *Fast facts.* www.mtroyal.ca/AboutMountRoyal/FastFacts/

Muehlenhard, C. L., Peterson, Z. D., Humphreys, T. P., & Johnson, K. N. (2017). Evaluating the one-in-five statistics: Women's risk of sexual assault while in college. *The Journal of Sex Research, 54*(4–5), 549–576. https://doi.org/10.1080/00224499.2017.1295014

Nasta, A., Shab, B., Brahmanandam, S., Richman, K., Wittels, K., Allsworth, J., & Boardman, L. (2005). Sexual victimization: Incidence, knowledge and resource use among a population of college women. *Journal of Pediatric and Adolescent Gynecology, 18*(2), 91–96. https//doi.org/10.1016/j.jpag.2005.01.002

New Brunswick Canada. (2019). *Now you know.* https://www2.gnb.ca/content/gnb/en/corporate/promo/sexual_violence.html

Office of the Press Secretary. (2014). *Memorandum: Establishing a white house task force to protect students from sexual assault.* https://obamawhitehouse.archives.gov/the-press-office/2014/01/22/memorandumestablishing-white-house-task-force-protect-students-sexual-a

Ostridge, L., & O'Connor, C. D. (2020). Reporting unwanted sexual behavior at a postsecondary institution: Student understandings of campus policy. *Canadian Journal of Family and Youth, 12*(1), 225–242. http://ejournals.library.ualberta.ca/index/php/cjfy

Paul, L. A., & Gray, M. J. (2011). Sexual assault programs on college campuses: Using social psychological belief and behavior change principles to improve outcomes. *Trauma, Violence & Abuse*, *12*(2), 99–109. www.jstor.org/stable/27010934

Phipps, A. (2010). Violent and victimized bodies: Sexual violence policy in England and Wales. *Critical Social Policy*, *30*(3), 359–383. https://doi.org/10.1177/0261018310367673

Pike, H. (2018, January 11). University of Calgary find they have "no grounds" to expel convicted sex offender. *Metro News*. www.metronews.ca/news/calgary/2018/01/11/university-of-calgary-find-they-have-no-grounds-to-expelconvicted-sex-offender.html

Potter, R. H., Krider, J. E., & McMahon, P. M. (2000). Examining elements of campus sexual violence policies: Is deterrence or health promotion favored? *Violence against Women*, *6*(12), 1345–1362. https://doi.org/10.1177/10778010022183686

Quam, S. (2017). Ending rape: Effective strategies for reducing sexual and relationship violence on a college campus. Syracuse University Honors Program Capstone Projects, 1028. https://surface.syr.edu/honors_capstone/1028

Quinlan, E., Clarke, A., & Miller, N. (2016). Enhancing care and advocacy for sexual assault survivors on Canadian campuses. *Canadian Journal of Higher Education*, *46*(2), 40–54. https://doi.org/10.47678/cjhe.v46i2.185184

Richards, T. N. (2016). An updated review of institutions of higher education's responses to sexual assault: Results from a nationally representative sample. *Journal of Interpersonal Violence*. https://doi.org/10.1177/0886260516658757

Royster. L. A. (2017). *Sexual violence prevention and response at institutions of higher education in a changing federal landscape: A feminist policy analysis* (ProQuest Dissertations Publishing). https://libres.uncg.edu/ir/uncg/listing.aspx?id=21960

Shankar, I. (2017, July 28). #Morethanhashtags: Universities should take concrete actions to end campus sexual violence. *Insider Higher Education*. www.insidehighered.com/advice/2017/07/28/universities-should-take-concrete-actionsstop-sexual-assault-essay

Shankar, I., & Tavcer, D. S. (2021). "Good people with good intentions": Deconstructing a post-secondary institution's sexual violence policy construction. *Canadian Journal of Educational Administration and Policy*, *195*, 2–16. https://doi.org/10.7202/1075669ar

Shen, A. (2017, August 4). Universities across Canada implement sexual violence policies. *University Affairs*. www.universityaffairs.ca/news/news-article/universities-across-canada-implement-sexual-violence-policies/

Smith, S. G., Basile, K. C., Gilbert, L. K., Merrick, M. T., Patel, N., Walling, M., & Jain, A. (2017). *National Intimate Partner and Sexual Violence Survey (NISVS): 2010–2012 state report*. National Center for Injury Prevention and Control, Centers for Disease Control and Prevention. www.researchgate.net/publication/317236957_The_National_Intimate_Partner_and_Sexual_Violence_Survey_NISVS_2010-2012_State_Report

St. Thomas University. (n.d.a). *Bystander intervention online training*. www.stu.ca/sexualviolencesupport/bystander-intervention-online-training-/

St. Thomas University. (n.d.b). *Home*. www.stu.ca

St. Thomas University. (n.d.c). *Sexual violence support & resources*. www.stu.ca/sexualviolencesupport/

Tougas, S., Naushan, A., & Patel, D. (2021). *Environmental scan of relevant GBV policies and law for Canadian post-secondary institutions*. Courage to Act: Addressing and Preventing Gender-Based Violence at Post-Secondary Institutions in Canada. www.couragetoact.ca/blog/environmental-scan

University of British Columbia (Okanagan Campus). (n.d.a). *Facts & figures*. https://ok.ubc.ca/about/facts-and-figures/

University of British Columbia (Okanagan Campus). (n.d.b). *Library: What is a land acknowledgement?* https://guides.library.ubc.ca/distance-research-xwi7xwa/landacknowledgements

University of British Columbia (Okanagan Campus). (n.d.c). Sexual violence prevention and response office. *We Believe You*. https://svpro.ok.ubc.ca

University of Ottawa. (n.d.a). *Incident of sexual violence: Online disclosure*. https://uoforms.uottawa.ca/sexual-violence-situation/en

University of Ottawa. (n.d.b). *Indigenous*. https://www2.uottawa.ca/about-us/indigenous

University of Ottawa. (n.d.c). *Sexual violence: Support and prevention: Training*. www.uottawa.ca/sexual-violence-support-and-prevention/training

University of Toronto. (2022). *The 2022 review of the policy on sexual violence and sexual harassment: Final report*. www.provost.utoronto.ca/wp-content/uploads/sites/155/2022/07/Final-Report_SVSHPolicyReview.pdf

University of Winnipeg. (n.d.a). *Fast facts*. www.uwinnipeg.ca/about/fast-facts/index.html

University of Winnipeg. (n.d.b). *Land acknowledgement*. www.uwinnipeg.ca/indigenous/land-acknowledgement.html

WESTAT. (2015). *Executive summary: Report on the AAU climate survey on sexual assault and sexual misconduct*. www.aau.edu/sites/default/files/%40%20Files/Climate%20Survey/Executive%20Summary%2012-14-15.pdf

Whittier, N. (2016). Where are the children? Theorizing the missing piece in gendered sexual violence. *Gender and Society, 30*(1), 95–108. www.jstor.org/stable/24756167

Wolitzky-Taylor, K. B., Resnick, H. S., Amstadter, A. B., McCauley, J. L., Ruggiero, K. J., & Kilpatrick, D. G. (2011). Reporting rape in a national sample of college women. *Journal of American College Health, 59*(7), 582–587. https://doi.org/10.1080/07448481.2010.515634

Wooten, S. C. (2015). Heterosexist discourses: How feminist theory shaped campus sexual violence policy. In R. W. Mitchell (Ed.), *The crisis of campus sexual violence: Critical perspectives on prevention and response* (Vol. 1, pp. 33–51). Routledge. www.taylorfrancis.com/chapters/edit/10.4324/9781315725604-3/heterosexist-discourses-sara-carrigan-wooten

Worthen, M.G.F. & Wallace, S. A. (2017). Intersectionality and perceptions about sexual assault education and reporting on college campuses. *Family Relations, 66*(1), 180–196. https://doi.org/10.1111/fare.12240

Yukon College. (2018). *HR-07 sexualized violence prevention and response policy*. www.yukonu.ca/sites/default/files/inline-files/HR-07%20Sexualized%20

116   *Policies and programming*

Violence%20Prevention%20and%20Response%20FINAL%20with%20
Appendix%208.1.pdf

Yukon University. (2018). *Sexualized violence prevention and response policy.*
www.yukonu.ca/sites/default/files/policies/HR%207.0%20-%20Sexualized%20
Violence%20Prevention%20and%20Response.0%20-%20Sexualized%20Vio-
lence%20Prevention%20and%20Response.pdf

The Yukon University Act SY 2019, c. 15. www.canlii.org/en/yk/laws/stat/sy-2019-c-
15/latest/sy-2019-c-15.html

5 Student voices

D. Scharie Tavcer and Vicky Dobkins

Introduction

Student participants were recruited during April–May 2020, then again in September–December 2020, and January–March 2021. The recruitment advert and anonymous link to the electronic survey were posted on the social media sites of the seven universities. Additional postings were on the PSI's student association or student group accounts (with permission) and shared with faculty and staff colleagues of Dr. Tavcer. Additional postings were on Dr. Tavcer's Twitter, Facebook, and LinkedIn accounts with relevant hashtags and tags. In total, 182 students completed the survey with an uneven distribution of participants among the seven PSIs: Concordia University (Québec); MacEwan University and Mount Royal University (Alberta); St. Thomas University (New Brunswick); the University of British Columbia Okanagan (British Columbia); the University of Winnipeg (Manitoba); and the University of Ottawa (Ontario).

Across these seven PSIs, electronic surveys and in-person interviewed combined for a total of 182 students – three students from University of British Columbia Okanagan, 89 from MacEwan University and Mount Royal University; 46 from the University of Winnipeg; one from the University of Ottawa; four from Concordia University and 14 from St. Thomas University. Prior to administering electronic surveys when the COVID-19 pandemic closed campuses, in-person interviews were conducted with 11 students and one staff at St. Thomas University, then three more students completed the electronic survey. Also prior to the pandemic, in-person interviews were conducted with 14 students and four staff from Mount Royal University. And over the phone, interviews were conducted with staff from Bow Valley College, the University of Calgary and MacEwan University (Alberta), the University of Victoria (British Columbia), Concordia University and McGill University (Québec), the University of Toronto (Ontario), the University of Winnipeg and

DOI: 10.4324/9781003332671-5

the University of Manitoba (Manitoba), and the University of Saskatchewan (Saskatchewan).

Combining all modes of data collection resulted in 198 total participants
(15 staff and 182 students).

Demographics

Two students checked off they were not over the age 18. Their data were not
included in the analysis as per the directions posted in the survey.

Of those students, 41 self-identified as male, 136 self-identified as female.
Others self-identified as "gender-queer," "non-binary," and three responded
with "question not relevant," or "prefer not to say."

Defining consent

One of the first questions in the survey asked students to share their understanding of consent. The literature provides evidence that most people
in Canada, including students, do not fully understand consent including
its legal definition and responsibilities. Our study aimed to uncover how
Canadian post-secondary students define consent with the hypothesis that
many get it wrong. One study discovered that "only 28% of people in
Canada fully understand what it means to give consent" (Canadian Wom-
en's Foundation, 2018). Their electronic survey included 1,502 randomly
selected Canadians aged 18 and over. Most studies come from the USA
and confirm that students are not educated about consent and rejection
(Muehlenhard et al., 2016; Weissbourd et al., n.d.). Addressing consent
starts with education and having evidence that education is needed, particularly in Canadian PSIs, can help PSIs to cater their prevention education strategies.

> *Question: How do you define consent for sexual activity?*
> *What does consent mean to you (legal or otherwise)?*

There was a wide variation in how students defined or explained their
understanding of consent, with legal concepts sometimes included. Some
answers were short such as *"explicitly saying yes"* or *"both people agree-
ing"* while others explained it in more details such as,

> *Consent is the permission given by an individual to follow through with
> desires. It must be given freely and consciously and can be reversed at
> anytime. Consent means respect to me. An individual can change their*

mind at any point without feeling obligated or forced to continue and the other person(s). Consent allows one to make the right decision for themselves and their body.

Consent is a very important agreement in terms of sexual activity. It is very simple to answer "yes" or "no" yet some individuals fail or ignore the answer and still proceed to do what they want. For me, consent is either you say "yes" if you are interested in doing something and "no" if you are not interested. Words such as " I don't know" or "I'm not sure" is still NO until the person verbally says "YES." This is extremely important for some people to understand because if the offender ends up taking steps then it can traumatize the victim in many ways and the offender can also face severe consequences.

consentmeans a straight up "yes." If my partner mumbles a half-hearted "yeah sure if you want . . ." I will ask again and be straight up, if he's not in the mood he's not in the mood.

Even if you are in a relationship I believe consent should matter. If your partner comes home drunk and has sex with you when you don't want to have sex. If the individual says no, anytime in the time questioned, it should still be sexual assault or rape.

saying the word YES. not being under duress or fear when participating in sexual activities.

Continually giving permission to engage in a sexual act, saying yes, and understanding that you can say no at any point if you are uncomfortable.

Saying or implying any disinterest means NO, physically saying yes means as such. Consent can also be revoked during intercourse meaning NO.

There were only a few problematic responses such as, "*I don't have to define it very often. Consent to me means two willing adults agree to be in an intimate and vulnerable situation with each other, and respect the agreement post sex. ie: someone can't take back or misuse the trust instilled post sex*" and "*Someone getting the yes or consensual body language*" indicating a reliance on myths and stereotypes" and "*willingness.*"

What's currently offered at your PSI?

The survey also queried what students know is happening at their PSIs about programming and services related to sexual violence prevention and consent education. And it asked how are those types of programming and services delivered?

> *Question: Please tell me what you know about your university's consent education programming . . . Check all that apply.*

What is offered?

Most students replied that they did not know what is being offered at their PSI. Most offered that programming and information are available on

Table 5.1 What type of consent education is offered at your university?

Mandatory in-person sessions.	6
Optional in-person sessions.	13
Mandatory online course/module.	3
Optional online course/module.	15
Posters and information adverts.	46
Student Association workshops (e.g., from your Pride Centre, Peer Support Centre, Indigenous Centre).	45
Occasional display booths and education campaigns.	11
Information in my courses and lectures.	8
Credit course that is in my Program or Degree.	3
Non-credit course that is offered from Continuing Education.	2
No idea/I am not aware of any programming.	17

Source: Author

Is consent important?

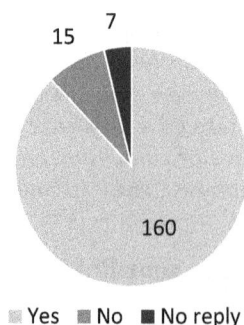

Figure 5.1 Students responding if consent education is important.
Source: Author.

posters and adverts with almost the same amount replying that programming is offered through Student Association workshops (e.g., from a Pride Centre, Peer Support Centre, Indigenous Centre), while others answered, "*No idea/I am not aware of any programming*" and others replied they were aware of in-person or online optional sessions only.

When is it offered?

Most students replied that consent education is offered only during new student orientation or during welcome week services, while others replied, "*No idea/I am not aware of any programming.*" And others responded that such education and programming can be received when requested.

Who gets consent education?

Most students replied either that such training is offered to everyone or that it is provided to those who ask for it only. Others indicated that it was part of other training for student leaders such as residence advisors or peer counsellors. Others replied that only students who attend new student orientation or student association workshops receive such training, while several others replied, "*No idea/I am not aware of any programming.*"

> *Question: Do you think it is important that your university has a consent education program or module?*

Over 90% of respondents said yes.

Should consent education be mandatory?

> Question: *Having read through the questions and viewed these slides, do you think an online sexual consent education module should be mandatory for all students at your university?*

Almost 90% (157 yes + 25 no; 86.26%) of respondents said yes, any consent education should be mandatory and gave their reasons.

> *Sexual assault rates are high in universities and people should be aware. because sometimes students are not aware about the information and laws of another country especially for foreign students.*

> *It should be mandatory because people should gain knowledge of this so they have no excuse later that they were unaware. And a way for victims to handle this situation.*

it should be mandatory to spread awareness.

Many classes in universities find a way to discuss consent, but not every class does, this would ensure that students are all getting the same education on such an important topic.

It should be mandatory because the more people know about this issue and all the information around it the closer we get to a safer world. Too many university students are subjected to sexual violence because the abuser doesn't know how to handle the rejection, the victim is too scared to say no, and way more.

Most university students are still teenagers or are pretty young. Rarely do people talk to us about consent or sex education. It's often learned from social media or in some cases, personal experience. Students often face mental health problems during school, putting them in a vulnerable place, where people can take advantage of their situation. They should be given the tool to protect themselves.

Whereas some students felt that it should not be mandatory:

I'm conflicted because I do think it should be mandatory but I also think it could be very triggering for some people so there needs to be an easy way to get out of it for those that could be triggered.

It shouldn't be mandatory, because people may not take it seriously/ may resent being made to complete it. I think that in-person training and education would be more beneficial.

I don't think the topic will be taken seriously if it is forced on students. Many will just get through it as quick as possible.

Mandatory for everyone?

Question: If the online sexual consent education module is mandatory for students, should everyone at your university have to take it?

Not just students but also the President, all the staff, all faculty, everyone?

Over 97% of respondents said yes it should be mandatory for everyone not just students.

Same as my answer to question 18. Also many people in power (mainly men, sorry to stereotype) dont understand the influence they have on those beneath them.

There are a lot of people in positions of authority that need to know about consent, and who should also be aware of what their student body knows about consent/sexual assault. Also, students will sometimes approach their professors for help with personal difficulties and experiences and professors should know how to help

Everyone needs to know what consent means. Everyone. No exceptions. Especially at an institution where both minors and adults attend.

It should be mandatory for everyone because it affects everyone, and these are the higher ups that could be at the head of the unfair power dynamics also discussed.

It's not just students who are being sexually assaulted – it can happen to anyone, anywhere. It's important for everyone to know and understand what to do if it does happen or if someone they know. Understanding how help those who have been through this type of experience is just as important and knowing how to help yourself. The more people who learn and understand this information, the more the stigma of sexual assault may be reduced. This information isn't there to scare people but it's available to help educate and hopefully, help people to make better decisions (ie: not take advantage of someone when they are under the influence of drugs or alcohol) and help those who have been through a sexual assault feel less alone.

It should be important for everone, including staff and faculty, because they would act as a support system for students who ever experience any sexual violence or rarely be the perpetrator and learn how it would affect the victims.

because it affects everyone; because everyone can be a victim; not everyone has an equal understanding of consent

Because this a community issue. Many people are violated and judged. Society still blames the victims

Table of contents

Through the research project, through literature and gathering best practices elsewhere, and through the surveys and interviews, a table of contents for this sexual consent module was created. It went through several iterations as we sought feedback from subject experts, practitioners, and students over various times. In the electronic survey, we showed students examples of slides, images, and content of an existing module and our proposed module and asked them for their input about what was included and what was also missing.

Quizzes

> Question: *Here's an example of what a mini quiz question might look like as you progress through the module. It asks about the 'stranger danger' myth, and users must choose an answer, and then information is provided to educate the user.*
>
> *What do you think about this? Should the online module have mini quizzes?*
>
> *Should users get all mini quizzes correct (10/10 for example)? What else?*

There was an even split in responses that the module should have mini quizzes embedded within it and the benefits and limitations of quizzes.

> *I DONT THINK PUTTING An score will help, maybe a test at the end of it. pass or fail*
>
> *I think the modules should not have mini quizes.*
>
> *Too much pressure to get 10/10 would not be good for people like me who stress over any test or quiz, I myself would not learn well if I had that pressure.*
>
> *Yes and yes!*
>
> *Quizzes are important to ensure individuals are not simply skipping through the content being offered. Requiring an entire understanding is necessary and I think the idea of showing where the misunderstanding may be is useful.*
>
> *I think it's really important to drive these important topics and to debunk these misconceptions of stranger danger, and that its important to highlight not to blame survivors of sexual assault; but I don't think that a mini quiz would do it justice. I feel there would be many factors that would get in the way, such as language barriers for those learning English.*
>
> *its good but I dont think you should need to get 10/10, sometimes questions are confusing and its not that you don't know the material. Would you have to redo the entire module if you get one wrong? Will you have to rewatch/reread all of the information without being able to click ahead even if you only got one wrong? If the 10/10 is meaning they pass all 10 mini quizzes and not referring to getting 100% on each one then I obviously think thats a good idea. ^^ proof that questions can be misunderstood.*

i don't think so by getting 10/10 is necessary important thing is everyone should aware about the information

I believe having a quiz wouldn't be the best idea. I think most people encounter consent and need to be aware of the information on how to deal with it and how to approach it. I don't think that a quiz should be necessary to learn about it. But if we did require a quiz I think the intervention should be a subject that is covered.

Online modules should have mini quizzes to ensure that people taking the course are paying attention and actually learning informations. I think users should definitely aim to get 100%, at the very least 80%.

If it's informational I don't think quizzes are necessary, if it's a mandatory or required course then yes. I think 10/10 should be the requirement but the answer shouldn't be given right after. They should have to go back and find the correct information/learn what they missed.

They should not have to get 10/10 but it should say the correct answer after they answer wrong

If it is simply for education and awareness purposes, there should not be any tests. Tests scare away people from actually participating because they may want to learn, but may not want to be tested on the material.

Power dynamics

Question: Should a consent education module include information about power dynamics?

Such as between staff and students, teachers and students, coaches, and athletes, between athletes etc.? Why or why not? What is important for us to consider? What is missing?

Overwhelming majority said yes that the topic of power dynamics should be included in any consent education.

Yes, there are still people who dont understand the idea of consent out of fear of repercussions. power imbalances play a big role in this.

This is important, but it's also a nuanced area. Information should include clarification on the nuances of power dynamics (eg; in a patriarchal society, women/trans folks carry less influence than some men but can still have consensual sex with them, and sometimes people with less social capital can abuse people with more capital)

Yes! Especially at institutions where both minors and adults attend. Relationships like that can be harmful especially to the person at disadvantage; a student dating a teacher could be forcing themselves to stay in the relationship in fear of failing the class.

No, although related I don't think power dynamics is part of consent. It is important to understand but I think it should be part of a different topic. It makes me think more towards gaining unfair advantage in academic integrity more so than consent. If it is to be included I think it should be coupled with how to say no or reject advances in a safe/ healthy/beneficial way.

Adults should be able to have consensual sex as long with who they want regardless of position.

yes!!! a lot of younger students don't understand how to recognize when a professor/staff member is acting inappropriately with them and they don't know who to go to either

Yes, because a lot of people put trust into people of power and may not realize there is such thing as power dynamics.

What else should be included?

There was an opportunity for students and staff to answer open-ended questions. One question asked what else should be included in a module. The majority of respondents agreed that any sexual consent education should include "how to handle rejection," "information about policies and processes," "information if I'm accused of sexual violence," "information for those victimised by sexual violence," "how to be an effective bystander," and "how to support someone who has disclosed sexual violence."

A written portion that is mandatory for reflection.

Advice for talking with peers who have sexually assaulted people, creating community support systems for victims of sexual abuse

I think a module about sexual assault while in a romantic relationship would be extremely important and helpful for many people, because not everyone realizes that you can be sexually assaulted while in a relationship. A relationship does not equal consent.

I believe older teens, should know about the book, in my late teens I was dating older men because I knew it would hurt my parents, rebellious stage and now looking back, not very smart. If, people knew that relationships werent "everything", maybe have a module about loving oneself, self image, so that when someone gives you attention you dont fall head over heels and throw everything away for an individual.

Childhood sexual assault

Consent between family

Resources to help those who need to actually discuss what consent is, rather than just taking a module.

should be a helpline number for 24 hours to report any incident related to sexual hay

Healthy kink negotiation and non-tramaresponses in kink and safewords, discuss multiple partners, and open relationships, normalize pauses in sex, especially if one partner is a victim of previous sexual assalut, and how sometimes everyone needs a pause to process a new feeling or emotion,

how to say no. because some people struggle with this, whether its the fear of what would happen if they said no or not wanting to come off a certain way.

What "counts" as sexual harassment/assault. I think there have a lot of people who have either committed or been victims of these things without realizing it because they don't think what happened "counts" as a violation of consent.

Talk about sexual coercion. Badgering someone until they feel forced to relent isn't exactly consent.

based on personal opinion, therapy should be highly recommended if said person fits the criteria. And I think the test should be done in one sitting; sexual assault is a very serious issue that affects a lot of people and you should go into the module with that in mind. It's not something you can shrug off and be like, "this is boring to me and I'll just finish it later."

I fell like some of those questions are unnecessary to have

Maybe how to recognize grooming and how to report it (this could be important for education teachers)

definition of consent/how consent is perceived in different parts of the world

As the responses reveal, students are invested in learning more about consent and are passionate that consent education should be included in their post-secondary education. They recognise that gaps in education exist and that some topics are often excluded in prevention education and support.

Intoxication and consent

The literature is rife with studies and commentary about the interconnectedness of drugs and alcohol and sexual violence and therefore it is imperative students be asked questions about this interconnection.

> *Question: What should and should not be included in an online consent education module*
>
> *about the topic of consent and intoxication?*
>
> *everything about consent!!! why some misudertandinshappen and how to communicate better*
>
> *When a person is intoxicated or under a drug, it is also important that the offender or individual understands that the other person is not in the right state of mind to give consent or any sexual help.*
>
> *Basically everything should be included in the topic that covers the topic of consent and intoxication.*
>
> *I think things such as drugs or alcohol being used should be shown and people slipping narcotics into people drinks. this stuff happens in real life so everyone should be aware*
>
> *This is a major topic that needs to be addressed because some people blame themselves because they were intoxicated. No still means no*
>
> *There is no such thing as consent when under the influence*
>
> *it should include facts, and it should not include biases.*
>
> *be cool, be smart, but be aware. know who you are hanging out with if you plan on drinking 5l of wine etc. know your limits but also, don't fear from having fun .*
>
> *Nothing should be left out of a consent module topic, all things intoxication*
>
> *intoxicated sex is going to happen, so saying intoxication prevents consent and ending it there does a huge disservice*

As the responses reveal, some students still subscribe to myths and stereotypes, but many students recognise the need for more discussion and education. Students are aware how intoxication conflates consent and also how important it is to education people that intoxication nullifies consent.

Other suggestions

Question: What do you think about a suggestions and tips slide?

Should the online module provide real-life scenarios as examples of what to say or do?

Would it be better if it was a video with real people role-playing

or are these faceless characters okay?

Some questions asked participants about the aesthetic layout and imagery in the sample slides for the proposed consent module.

Good. Real life scenarios are good, some people don't know how to act so the role playing aspect could be helpful. I still think faceless characters are fine. But if faces are important then use cartoon people maybe.

i think videos with role playing characters are more beneficial and advantages because people like to watch videos and they can understand the situation more accurately.

Advice for talking with peers who have sexually assaulted people, creating community support systems for victims of sexual abuse

I think examples are good; however, some people will take this as a script which wouldn't be appropriate in every situation. Not much can be done in that regard other than trying to offer several examples to encompass more situations. I think faceless characters are good. I don't think you need to be able to tell or even guess what gender they are. They should just be cartoon/stick people like; someone is bound to be offended that it is a rather heteronormative looking pair of shadows. Videos would be good as well

Faceless characters would be good. Personally, I think having to watch extra videos on top of the information can be a deterent for a voluntary course.

Real life scenarios are definitleythe way to go because that's reality. You can't give a course on this type of topic without giving real life examples. It might be tough to hear but this course would prepare people (as much as possible) for the scenarios if they were to ever occur. I also feel people will remember the scenario better and how to respond if they have real life characters to relate to.

Yes I think online modules should provide real-life scenarios as they can be extremely helpful. Especially if one of those scenarios happens to you in the future. I think a video with real people role-playing would seem more realistic and overall more useful than faceless characters because you can get a sense of how the scenarios might go if it were to happen in real life.

No situation is the same!!!! Role play is almost useless. Every person is different. This also doesn't help for people who speak other languages, different cultures.

Yes real-life examples, or (unfortunately) common instances would help people prepare/identify the common markers. I think faceless are okay, with voice over?

I think it should definitely include the consequences of not gaining ones consent and the harm it causes. Scenarios would be interesting – "what would you do in this situation?"

role-playing videos of this sort of content always look staged and awkward, and often detract from the message being presented. suggestions and tips should be included, as well as scenario examples as above, an ideal module would have options for both text based and video scenarios, of which the student can decide which to engage with.

Conclusion

This chapter was informed by students and staff at the seven PSIs of focus. Although generally informed, there is room for growth in educating students about consent. The research also confirms the literature that students want consent education, and they want to discuss the difficult topics within it. Students also confirm that not just students should be educated about consent in that they realise the entire campus community needs to be learned about SV, consent, bystander intervention, and supporting others.

References

Canadian Women's Foundation. (2018, May 16). *Survey finds drop in Canadians' understanding of consent.* https://canadianwomen.org/survey-finds-drop-in-canadians-understanding-of-consent/#:~:text=We%20empower%20women%20and%20girls,women's%20foundations%20in%20the%20world

Muehlenhard, C. L., Jozkowski, K. N., Peterson, Z. D., & Humphreys, T. (2016). The complexities of sexual consent among college students: A conceptual and empirical review. *The Journal of Sex Research, 53*(4), 1–31. https://doi.org/10.10 80/00224499.2016.1146651

Weissbourd, R., Anderson, T. R., Cashin, A., & McIntyre, J. (n.d.). *The Talk: How adults can promote young people's healthy relationships and prevent misogyny and sexual harassment.* Harvard Graduate School of Education. https://static1. squarespace.com/static/5b7c56e255b02c683659fe43/t/5bd51a0324a69425bd0 79b59/1540692500558/mcc_the_talk_final.pdf

6 The online module

D. Scharie Tavcer and Vicky Dobkins

Introduction

Canadian students deserve safe spaces when they are at post-secondary institutions (PSIs), an environment where everyone understands and respects consent. In assisting with PSI's efforts, a #cultureofconsent recognises and addresses the systemic issues that perpetuate and reinforce SV with the potential to break the cycle of rape culture or the culture of silence. The literature, along with advocacy groups, has conceded that establishing a culture that respects and supports consent should be centred on "mutual understanding, knowledge, and agreement of each other's boundaries and limitations" (CFS – Ontario, n.d.; Ontario Tech University, 2020, para. 6).

Throughout this book, it has been reiterated repeatedly that the SV prevalence and reporting rates in Canada have not subsided in over 30 years. And the research has typically centred on white, cisgender, heteronormative sexual narratives which have resulted in programming that focuses only on female victims and is not inclusive of those who identify as Indigenous, racialised, gender diverse, and/or with visible and invisible disabilities (Humphreys & Towl, 2020; Solomon, 2018; SVPC, 2017). We need to do SV prevention and education differently. One way to shift attitudes and beliefs about SV from one of tolerance to safety and respect is through the development and implementation of sexual consent education (SVPC, 2017).

This book is a culmination of the results of the research project and this chapter presents one outcome, an online sexual consent module for post-secondary students. This module's foundation is based on the work of Concordia University's module *It Takes All of Us: Creating a Campus Community Free of Sexual Violence.*[1] Then, it grew, and we expanded to include the best practices from across Canada and from across various sources.

The sexual consent module envisioned here is titled Consent 101. It is designed to be an introduction to consent, SV, and the various ways to support

DOI: 10.4324/9781003332671-6

students. It is designed with students as the primary user, but it can be adapted for employee users. Consent 101 is an online module that was developed to be a multi-pronged approach to prevention education and is *not* intended to be a stand-alone prevention, education, or intervention, nor should it be offered on an ad hoc basis. The research project confirmed that students want consent education, they want consent education to include a variety of topics, and they want it to be mandatory for students, staff, and administrators at PSIs. Therefore our premise is that the Consent 101 module should be made mandatory, should be added to the repertoire of other prevention, education, and intervention efforts, and it should be expanded to include employees too.

The basics

Trauma-informed practice

There is recognition among professionals of the importance of adopting a trauma-informed approach to any education or intervention programming (Benoit et al., 2015; Colpitts, 2019; Salvino et al., 2017; SVPC, 2017). A trauma-informed approach in SV work acknowledges the widespread impact of the trauma of SV and integrates that knowledge and awareness into policies, procedures, and practices (EVABC, 2016). It seeks to ensure that the prevention and support programmes implemented respect the wishes of survivors and reduce retraumatisation (Salvino et al., 2017; SVPC, 2017). Key practices of trauma-informed sexual consent education move away from teaching from a place of fear, shame, and blame, towards approaches with additional care, sensitivity, and inclusivity (Action Canada SHR, 2020).

Accessibility

Because the module is an online platform, accessibility features can be interwoven within it such as closed captioning for the visually impaired, computer-generated narration in varying tones and pitches for the hearing impaired, including a text version of the entire module's script, as well as offering the narration in different languages.

Support

Because students may be triggered, unsettled, angered, provoked, or challenged by the content, the Consent 101 online module includes an "I'm feeling overwhelmed" button (see Figure 6.1) on every slide and can be used at any time to pause the module and to direct users to on-campus and off-campus supports and resources as well as live or 24-hour support services links.

Learn more

Each slide also includes a button where users can be directed to scholarly material to learn more about the topic discussed.

Navigation

Another slide offers users instructions on how to navigate the module and its various components (see Figure 6.3).

Intersectionality

While SV impacts all members of society, it may disproportionately affect members of social groups who experience intersecting forms of systemic discrimination or barriers (Salvino et al., 2017). The prevalence of SV on campuses is well researched yet perspectives that focus on intersectionality have been largely overlooked (Worthen & Wallace, 2017). Intersectionality is a term that describes the interconnected nature of all forms of oppression (cultural, institutional, and social) against particular groups (Canadian Federation of Students – Ontario, n.d.). It requires the analysis of how systemic power, privilege, oppression, and social location work together to mediate an individual's lived experiences (Almeida et al., 2019; Colpitts, 2019; Crenshaw, 1989; Salvino et al., 2017).

Most campus SV education programmes are designed for heteronormative and cisgender individuals, or predominantly directed at potential victims only, all of which signifies a need for more evidence-based queries of intersectionality with regard to student awareness, perceptions of reporting, and responses to campus sexual consent education (Worthen & Wallace, 2017). Every effort to address SV should be grounded within an

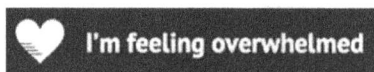

Figure 6.1 I'm feeling overwhelmed button.

Source: Author and design team.

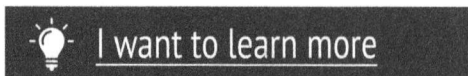

Figure 6.2 I want to learn more button.

Source: Author and design team.

Figure 6.3 How do I use this thing? (The sexual violence continuum which is referenced in part 1 of the module)

Source: Author and design team.

intersectional approach (Salvino et al., 2017). An intersectional approach recognises that different aspects of an individual's identity interact to influence their navigation, opportunities, and experiences. And certain groups do not feel safe while interacting with police and security personnel, authority figures from their PSIs, and support staff due to systemic discrimination and mistreatment (Buss et al., 2016; Salvino et al., 2017). An intersectional approach is incorporated into every element of the Consent 101 module as it informs every aspect of what sustains SV in Canada.

The learning aims

To address SV from students' perspectives as possible victims and potential perpetrators, as well as including best practices collated through the research project, the module encompasses five learning aims.

(1) Normalising the discussion about sexual violence and consent.
(2) Confronting any stereotypes and myths about sexual violence and consent.
(3) Increasing the understanding of giving and receiving consent.
(4) Educating participants about resources, policies, and processes.
(5) Building up skills to enforce a consent culture across all campus communities.

The Consent 101 module is divided into four parts with each having learning aims.

Part I: Understanding sexual violence

Part I learning aims:

•   To understand what is sexual violence and why it happens?
•   To learn the facts about sexual violence.
•   And to confront myths and stereotypes.

Part I provides a comprehensive understanding of sexual violence, how it is defined in law, and why it happens. Sexual violence transpires on a continuum of expression (see Figure 6.3). A continuum is a series of events or steps that seep into the next and they all share an underlying characteristic.

SV is informed by colonialism, patriarchy, toxic masculinity, misogyny, homophobia, and other structural inequities and violence against Indigenous people have been the subject of ongoing analysis, commentary, and community-based interventions by Indigenous educators and activists (EVABC, 2016; Native Women's Association of Canada, 2011). SV is rooted in our colonial history and a patriarchal culture that supports toxic masculinity. This harms not only girls and women, trans people, or people on the 2SLGBTQIA+ rainbow, but it also harms boys and men. It teaches boys and men that they must be socially dominant, financially successful, sexually experienced, and heterosexual which connects to other cultural norms such as misogyny and homophobia. All of this is "toxic" because it promotes violence, and it does not allow boys and men to be who they want to be. Instead, they must fit into a socially prescribed gendered box. Policymakers and educators must question how patriarchal discourses inform their own and others' understandings of violence, consent, victims, perpetrators, and fair judicial processes (Garcia & Vemuri, 2017).

SV is produced within a patriarchal culture and the root cause of it lies in misogyny (Beres, 2020). Rape culture also has deep roots in misogyny, and this male-dominated world has led people to believe they are lesser (Cusmano, 2018). The structural violence of rape culture can be understood as "produced by the cultural violence that is the ideological commitment to misogyny, chivalry, and the devaluation of men and women who live outside of prescribed gender scripts" (Nicholls, 2021, p. 39). Rape culture is another cultural norm that explains why the prevalence rates of SV have not changed in 30 years.

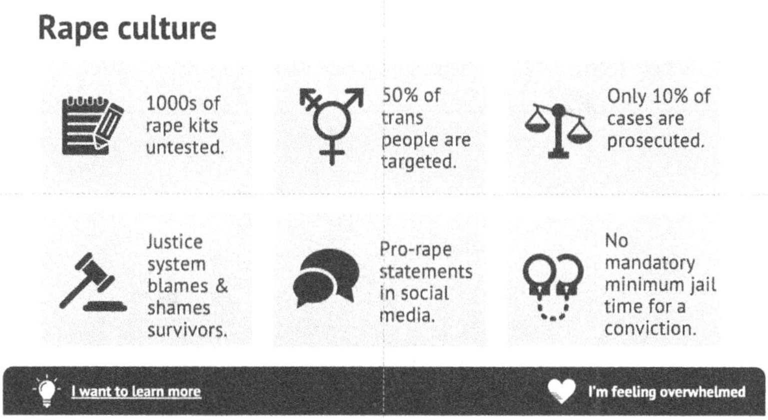

Rape culture

Figure 6.4 The impacts of rape culture
Source: Author and design team.

Part II: Understanding sexual consent

The learning aims for Part II:

- To define and explain consent.
- To understand the intersectional issues that influence a person's ability to give and receive consent.
- To learn how to ask for consent and learn ways to deal with rejection.

Part II sets out to provide an understanding of the intersectional issues that influences a person's ability to give and receive consent as well as ways to ask for consent and how to deal with rejection. Understanding consent in the context of sex can be convoluted. And there are certain factors, invisible things that lurk beneath the surface, that can impact our ability to give consent as well as the willingness to receive consent. These underlying factors can be best explained using the metaphor of an iceberg (see Figure 6.5) as a pictorial example of underlying factors such as poverty, disability, a language barrier, precarious immigration status, and more.

Below the surface are power dynamics at play. Power can be visible or invisible, overt, or subtle. Power can show up as power over others, power with others, and/or power within or outside of a group. A person in a position of power, authority, or trust (e.g., teacher, coach, counsellor, boss) can misuse their authority to coerce or force a person to engage in sexual activity) (Basile et al., 2014), and coercion intersects with power, race, ability, and social economic status.

People who perpetuate SV also target vulnerability. A "lower" position of power, financial power versus poverty, housed versus unhoused, employed versus unemployed, all of this can impact a person's ability to give consent.

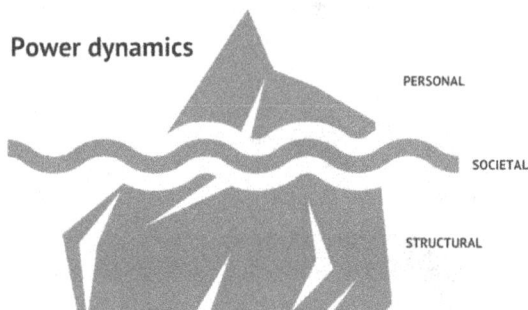

Figure 6.5 The consent iceberg.
Source: Author and design team.

SV is an act of aggression committed by those who are more powerful against those who are less powerful (EVABC, 2016). Institutional power may be embodied by professors or structures and processes within a university and SV policies should address how such positions influence or maintain negative or retraumatising environments for students (see Figure 6.6).

Consent and intoxication carry myths and patriarchal beliefs, such as if a person who is assaulted is a woman, they are shamed and blamed because they were intoxicated. Discussing intoxication and sex in any educational context is not an easy endeavour. In some cases, young people consider it passé or even an expected part of campus life. In other situations, drinking is often central to socialising, and others may feel peer-pressured and could be at risk of sexual predators that utilise alcohol as a weapon (Jacobs, 2021; Martell Consulting Services Ltd., 2014). But research confirms that many sexual assaults, particularly among young people, involve alcohol and/or drugs. Alcohol and/or drugs do not cause sexual assault, but they are a contributing factor to SV (Haskell, 2011; Martell Consulting Services Ltd., 2014). Alcohol and drugs are used to justify criminal behaviour and blame those who are targeted rather, it increases a person's vulnerability for someone who wishes to target them. Perpetrators use drugs and alcohol to decrease resistance from the person they are assaulting. Perpetrators use drugs or alcohol to make a target vulnerable, ensuring that the survivor may not recall enough details about the assault to tell the police. Perpetrators use drugs and alcohol as an excuse to say it lowers their inhibitions to excuse their actions or make it more challenging to hear and see the "no" cues.

Power dynamics

Senior versus junior player. Coach versus athlete. Professor versus student. Landlord versus tenant. Manager versus employee.

I want to learn more   I'm feeling overwhelmed

Figure 6.6 Power dynamics.
Source: Author and design team.

Our culture's fixation with drugs and alcohol and sexual assault is a perfect example of rape culture. Think of how many "tips" revolve around this subject: Cover your drink, have your friends watch over your drink, or never accept drinks from strangers. In fact, some people might say you just should not get drunk at all because it makes you more vulnerable to sexual assault. It perpetuates rape culture which believes that rape is inevitable and that people should do things to protect themselves, rather than redirect prevention efforts at potential perpetrators.

Another area that is missing from many preventions or education programmes, is how to handle rejection, and directed at potential perpetrators. Being rejected can be devastating, including the fear of rejection. Within the context of sexual consent, the topic of rejection has gendered dimensions where a culture rife with toxic masculinity does not allow men to be rejected. Society labels them as weak or as losers if they do. This pushes men to keep pestering and persuading until they get the response they want. It teaches them not to take no for an answer. This, unfortunately, can lead to violence. There is also the fear that rejecting the advances of another person can result in the escalation of violence. In fact, we see cases in the news of someone beating or killing the person who has rejected them or left a relationship.

We need to make it okay for all men to support each, not shame each other when they are rejected. We need to shift things so that people are not afraid something bad will happen if they say no.

Part III: Helping others

The learning aims of part III include the following:

- To understand what it means to be a bystander and the ways in which you can choose to be a bystander.
- To accept that people are impacted by sexual violence in diverse ways.
- To consider the barriers that prevent people from reporting or seeking support.
- And to learn how we can properly respond to people who seek help and support.

Part III brings attention to different methods of helping others and helping oneself. This can include bystander intervention (see Figure 6.7) or responding to disclosures. Bystander intervention programs (BIPs) teach participants how to intervene safely when an act of SV is happening, they also guide how to assist people and teach skills to support a friend or loved one who discloses victimisation (Lonsway et al., 2009; Mazar, 2019).

Bystander intervention

Then, choose a strategy.

- Distract
- Direct
- Delegate
- Document
- Delay

I want to learn more

I'm feeling overwhelmed

Figure 6.7 Bystander interventions.
Source: Author and design team.

People are impacted by SV and can have serious immediate or long-term consequences. We know that experiencing SV can impact a person's relationships and intimacy, work, school, self-esteem, emotions, physical health, and mental health, including, but not limited to, anxiety, shock, fear, anger, shame, guilt, depression, isolation, nightmares, flashbacks, difficulty concentrating or sleeping, post-traumatic stress, eating disorders, substance use, self-harm, suicidal ideation and attempts, and more (Brennan & Taylor-Butts, 2008; Chen & Ullman, 2010; Cotter & Savage, 2019; Cybulska, 2007; Haskell & Randall, 2019; Littleton et al., 2006).

Everyone responds differently and there is no one way or correct way to respond to being a victim of SV. SV also impacts the friends and family of those who are targeted, as well as the friends and family of the perpetrators too. In many ways, everyone is impacted by SV which confirms it is a societal issue.

There are numerous reasons why people do not want to report their assault (either to police or to loved ones) and those can include the internalisation of shame, guilt, or stigma (Cotter & Savage, 2019; Johnson, 2012; Sable et al., 2006), fear of reprisals, worrying about upsetting friends or family, or feeling overwhelmed by the judicial process or other formal reporting avenues, or more. Some people have conflicted feelings about the perpetrator, particularly when the perpetrator is a partner or a friend of the family.

Trouble remembering details can be a barrier to disclosing the attack or seeking help too. Trauma affects the brain's ability to file memories. Add drugs or alcohol, and a person's memory becomes more compromised. Perpetrators rely on this. Only one in ten sexual assaults get reported to police not because they did not happen but because our society does not support victims to come forward. People are hesitant to disclose especially if they are a marginalised or racialised person, or someone with a disability or language barrier, or precarious work or immigration status. They fear no one will believe them or that there will be other consequences. Society reinforces the myth that all SV is committed by strangers and should come with physical injuries, so when someone's experience differs from that, we question whether their experience "counts" as SV (see Figure 6.8). All these things prevent survivors from coming forward and seeking help. And perpetrators use these myths to assault others with impunity.

Responding to disclosures is another important part of any consent education programming. There is no one perfect recipe for supporting someone. But if PSIs can work in little and big ways to create a #cultureofconsent through trauma-informed policies, programming, education, and messaging, it can create safe spaces. Giving support, listening with empathy, and sharing resources, offering specialised training, can be helpful starting points (see Figure 6.9). Whether a person wants to report their victimisation to school authorities or police, and just as important is for PSIs to have supports and

People are impacted by sexual violence

shame, fear, anger, guilt, isolation, nightmares, flashbacks, difficulty concentrating or sleeping, anxiety, depression, post-traumatic stress disorder, substance overuse, eating disorders, self-harm, suicidal ideation & attempts, over work, and more...

I want to learn more   I'm feeling overwhelmed

Figure 6.8 People are impacted by sexual violence.

Source: Author and design team.

How do I respond to a disclosure?

CALM

create safety

ask appropriate questions

listen

make connections

💡 <u>I want to learn more</u>   ♥ I'm feeling overwhelmed

Figure 6.9 C.A.L.M. Create safety, Ask appropriate questions, Listen, Make connections.

Source: Author and design team.

resources available for perpetrators who want help to be accountable for their behaviour.

Part IV: Community and support

The learning aims for part IV include the following:

- Provide users with helping resources for victims and perpetrators.
- Provide resources that are on and off campus.
- Illustrate what happens when a report is made to the PSI or to the police.

It is imperative that education programming includes unpacking how policies will work if someone chooses to report SV (see Figure 6.9), seek help for being targeted, and seek help for accountability for being a perpetrator. Education programming needs to clarify the policy's scope on or off campus if the perpetrator is a campus student, employee, or not, and who will be involved once a report or disclosure is made, including the difference between a disclosure and a report to university authorities versus external authorities such as the police. Each university may have a different reporting process with outcomes (see Figure 6.10 for an example).

What happens if I report

Report of sexual violence · Assessment · Investigation · Adjudication · Final decision · Interim measures · (possible) Appeal

I want to learn more   I'm feeling overwhelmed

Figure 6.10 What happens if I report . . .
Source: Author and design team.

Conclusion

The conclusion of the module includes an evaluation of students' understanding of what they learned. At the start of the module, students are asked 13 questions and the same questions are offered at the conclusion of the module. The evaluation "tests" how the learning aims for each part have been achieved and also provides the opportunity for students to give open-ended feedback.

Also offered at the completion of the module is the opportunity for users to receive a certificate of completion. Students surveyed in this research project generally felt that receiving such certification would benefit them in practicum or future employment applications. A certificate of completion can also be used to track users should the PSI wish to make the module mandatory.

Calls to action

Each part concludes with calls to action – ideas and suggestions for students to further support a culture of consent on campus, in their communities, and at home. The list is not exhaustive but is a starting point for students to consider.

Part I calls to action

- Examine, challenge, and change your own beliefs and behaviours.
- Don't use objectifying or degrading language.

- Shut down victim blaming and shaming.
- Speak out if you hear an offensive joke.
- Share facts (not myths) about sexual violence and consent.
- Take care of yourself and others.

Part II calls to action

- Speak out if you witness someone abusing their position of power over another person.
- Normalise conversations about consent.
- Never assume consent.
- Talk about & model how to handle rejection with your friends, family, partners, kids, nieces/nephews, grandkids.

Part III calls to action

- Thank you for telling me.
- I believe you.
- Would it be helpful to talk to a counsellor?
- What can I do to help?
- I'm here to support you.

Part IV calls to action

- Join the Dating, Domestic, and Sexual Violence Committee (DDSVC), peer support groups, and relevant social media accounts from MRU and other support agencies.
- Learn about and tell others about MRU's policies and procedures.
- Learn about and tell others about the Survivor/Victim Bill of Rights.
- Sign up for workshops.

Note

1 Concordia University's consent program, *It Takes All of Us*, is based upon expertise provided by Jennifer Drummond, the Sexual Assault Resource Centre Coordinator at Concordia University, and other contributors, and was developed by Knowledge One, Concordia University's online education service provider.

References

Action Canada SHR. (2020, April 3). *The state of sex-ed in Canada*. https://www.actioncanadashr.org/sites/default/files/2019-09/Action%20Canada_Stateof SexEd_F%20-%20web%20version%20EN.pdf

Almeida, R. V., Werkmeister Rozas, L. M., Cross-Denny, B., Lee, K. K., & Yamada, A.-M. (2019). Coloniality and intersectionality in social work education and practice. *Journal of Progressive Human Services, 30*(2), 148–164. https://doi.org/10. 1080/10428232.2019.1574195

Basile, K., Smith, S., Breiding, M., Black, M., & Mahendra, R. (2014). *Sexual violence surveillance: Uniform definitions and recommended data elements.* www. cdc.gov/violenceprevention/pdf/sv_surveillance_definitionsl-2009-a.pdf

Benoit, C., Shumka, L., Phillips, R., Kennedy, M. C., & Belle-Isle, L. (2015, December). Issue brief: Sexual violence against women in Canada. *Status of Women Canada.* https://cfc-swc.gc.ca/svawc-vcsfc/index-en.html

Beres, M. (2020). Perspectives of rape-prevention educators on the role of consent in sexual violence prevention. *Sex Education, 20*(2), 227–238. https://doi.org/10. 1080/14681811.2019.1621744

Brennan, S., & Taylor-Butts, A. (2008, December). Sexual assault in Canada, 2004 and 2007. Canadian Centre for Justice Statistics. Profile Series. No. 19. (Statistics Canada Catalogue no. 85F0033M). https://www150.statcan.gc.ca/n1/en/pub/85f0033m/85f0033m2008019-eng.pdf?st=rxS14fst

Buss,D.,Majury,D.,Moore,D.,Rigakos,G.S.,&Singh,R.(2016,June).Theresponsetosexual *violence at Ontario university campuses: Final report.* www.academia.edu/32063786/ The_Response_to_Sexual_Violence_at_Ontario_University_Campuses

Canadian Federation of Students – Ontario. (n.d.). *Campus toolkit for creating consent culture.* https://cfsontario.ca/wp-content/uploads/2017/07/Consent-Toolkit.pdf

Chen, Y., & Ullman, S. E. (2010). Women's reporting of sexual and physical assaults to police in the national violence against women survey. *Violence against Women, 16*(3), 262–279. https://journals.sagepub.com/doi/pdf/10.1177/1077801209360861

Colpitts, E. M. (2019). *An intersectional analysis of sexual violence policies, responses, and prevention efforts at Ontario universities* (Dissertation). https:// yorkspace.library.yorku.ca/xmlui/handle/10315/36778

Cotter, A., & Savage, L. (2019, December 5). Gender-based violence and unwanted sexual behaviour in Canada, 2018: Initial findings from the survey of safety in public and private spaces. *Juristat* (Statistics Canada Catalogue no. 85–002-X). https://www150.statcan.gc.ca/n1/pub/85-002-x/2019001/article/00017-eng.htm

Crenshaw, K. (1989). Demarginalizing the intersection of race and sex: A black feminist critique of antidiscrimination doctrine, feminist theory and antiracist politics. *University of Chicago Legal Forum, 1989*(1), 139–167. https://chicagounbound. uchicago.edu/cgi/viewcontent.cgi?article=1052&context=uclf

Cusmano, D. (2018). Rape culture rooted in patriarchy, media portrayal, and victim blaming. *Writing Across the Curriculum, 30.* https://digitalcommons.sacredheart. edu/wac_prize?utm_source=digitalcommons.sacredheart.edu%2Fwac_prize% 2F30&utm_medium=PDF&utm_campaign=PDFCoverPages

Cybulska, B. (2007). Sexual assault: Key issues. *Journal of the Royal Society of Medicine, 100*(7), 321–324. https://doi.org/10.1177/014107680710000713

Ending Violence British Columbia (EVABC). (2016, May). Sexual assault support worker handbook. https://endingviolence.org/publications/sexual-assault-support-worker-handbook/

Garcia, C., & Vemuri, A. (2017). Theorizing "rape culture": How law, policy, and education can support and end sexual violence. *Education & Law Journal*, *27*(1), 1–17. www.proquest.com/scholarly-journals/theorizing-rape-culture-how-law-policy-education/docview/1983614241/se-2

Haskell, L. (2011). Key best practices for effective sexual violence public education campaigns: A summary. *Queen's Printer for Ontario*. https://studylib.net/doc/18249686/key-best-practices-for-ef

Haskell, L., & Randall, M. (2019). *The impact of trauma on adult sexual assault victims: What the criminal justice system needs to know*. https://papers.ssrn.com/sol3/papers.cfm?abstract_id=3417763

Humphreys, C. J., & Towl, G. J. (2020). *Addressing student sexual violence in higher education: A good practice guide*. Emerald Publishing Limited.

Jacobs, S. (2021, September 14). *Working together to end the red zone*. http://uwimprint.ca/article/working-together-to-end-the-red-zone/

Johnson, H. (2012). Limits of a criminal justice response: Trends in police and court processing of sexual assault. In E. A. Sheehy (Ed.), *Sexual assault in Canada: Law, legal practice and women's activism* (pp. 613–634). University of Ottawa Press. https://books.openedition.orgupp/592

Littleton, H. L., Axsom, D., Breitkopf, C. R., & Berenson, A. (2006). Rape acknowledgment and postassault experiences: How acknowledgment status relates to disclosure, coping, worldview, and reactions received from others. *Violence and Victims*, *21*(6), 761–778. https://doi.org/10.1891/vv-v21i6a00

Lonsway, K. A., Banyard, V. L., Berkowitz, A. D., Gidycz, C. A., & Katz, J. T. (2009). Rape prevention and risk reduction: Review of the research literature for practitioners. *The National Online Resource Center on Violence against Women*. https://vawnet.org/material/rape-prevention-and-risk-reduction-review-research-literature-practitioners

Martell Consulting Services Ltd. (2014). *Student safety in Nova Scotia: A review of student union policies and practices to prevent sexual violence*. www.studentsns.ca/s/2014-05-09-sexual-assault-report-KB-for-web1.pdf

Mazar, L. (2019). History and theoretical understanding of bystander intervention. In W. T. O'Donohue & P. A. Schewe (Eds.), *Handbook of sexual assault and sexual assault prevention* (pp. 423–432). Springer. https://doi.org/10.1007/978-3-030-23645-8

Native Women's Association of Canada. (2011). *Aboriginal lateral violence*. www.nwac.ca/assets-knowledge-centre/2011-Aboriginal-Lateral-Violence.pdf

Nicholls, T. (2021). *Dismantling rape culture: The peacebuilding power of "Me Too"*. Routledge. https://library.oapen.org/handle/20.500.12657/42839

Ontario Tech University. (2020, February 12). *Establishing a culture of consent on campus*. https://community.ontariotechu.ca/blog/awareness/establishing-a-culture-of-consent-on-campus.php

Sable, M. R., Danis, F., Mauzy, D. L., & Gallagher, S. K. (2006). Barriers to reporting sexual assault for women and men: Perspectives of college students. *Journal of American College Health*, *55*(3), 157–162.

Salvino, C., Gilchrist, K., & Cooligan-Pang, J. (2017). *OurTurn: A national action plan to end campus sexual violence*. https://ssmu.ca/wp-content/uploads/2018/03/our_turn_action_plan_final_english_web2.pdf?x26516#:~:text=Our%20Turn%20is%20

a%20national,our%20university%20and%20college%20campuses.&text=The%20
way%20the%20Our%20Turn,may%20adopt%20only%20a%20few

Sexual Violence Prevention Committee (SVPC). (2017, December 15). *Changing
the culture of acceptance: Recommendations to address sexual violence on university campuses.* Council of Nova Scotia University Presidents. https://novascotia.
ca/lae/pubs/docs/changing-the-culture-of-acceptance.pdf

Solomon, A. H. (2018, August 10). Talking to college students about "the red zone".
Psychology Today. www.psychologytoday.com/ca/blog/loving-bravely/201808/
talking-college-students-about-the-red-zone

Worthen, M. G. F., & Wallace, S. A. (2017). Intersectionality and perceptions about
sexual assault education and reporting on college campuses. *Family Relations,
66*(1), 180–196. https://doi.org/10.1111/fare.12240

Index

Note: Page numbers in *italics* indicate a figure, in **bold** indicate a table, and in ***bold italics*** indicate a box on the corresponding page.

For Product Safety Concerns and Information please contact our EU
representative GPSR@taylorandfrancis.com
Taylor & Francis Verlag GmbH, Kaufingerstraße 24, 80331 München, Germany

www.ingramcontent.com/pod-product-compliance
Lightning Source LLC
Chambersburg PA
CBHW061741270326
41928CB00011B/2331

9 781032 365657